G000298932

THE ISLAND SERIES

ST KILDA

AND OTHER HEBRIDEAN OUTLIERS

OTHER SCOTTISH TITLES FROM DAVID & CHARLES

General

Orkney and Shetland: An Archaeological Guide
Scotland: A New Study
Scotland: The Shaping of a Nation
Walking Through Scotland
The Munros in Winter
100 Best Routes on Scottish Mountains

Islands

Island of Bute
Isle of Arran
Kintyre
Shetland
Skye
Staffa
Uists and Barra

Transport

Classic Scottish Paddle Steamers
The Clyde Puffer
Forgotten Railways: Scotland
The North British Railway, Vols 1 and 2
A Regional History of the Railways of Great Britain: Vol 6
  Scotland: The Lowlands and the Borders
The West Highland Railway

ST KILDA
AND OTHER HEBRIDEAN OUTLIERS

FRANCIS THOMPSON

DAVID & CHARLES
Newton Abbot London North Pomfret (Vt)

British Library Cataloguing in Publication Data

Thompson, Francis, *1931–*
St. Kilda and other Hebridean outliers.
New. ed.—(The Islands series).
1. Scotland. Western Isles, to 1988
I. Title II. Series
941.1'4

ISBN 0–7153–9214–X

First published 1970
New edition 1988

© Francis Thompson 1970, 1988

All rights reserved. No part of this
publication may be reproduced, stored
in a retrieval system, or transmitted,
in any form or by any means, electronic,
mechanical, photocopying, recording or
otherwise, without the prior permission
of David & Charles Publishers plc

Printed in Great Britain
by Redwood Burn Ltd, Trowbridge, Wilts
for David & Charles Publishers plc
Brunel House Newton Abbot Devon

Published in the United States of America
by David & Charles Inc
North Pomfret Vermont 05053 USA

To

Rona, Ewan, Fay and Eilidh,
who will one day visit these islands

CONTENTS

ILLUSTRATIONS

IN TEXT

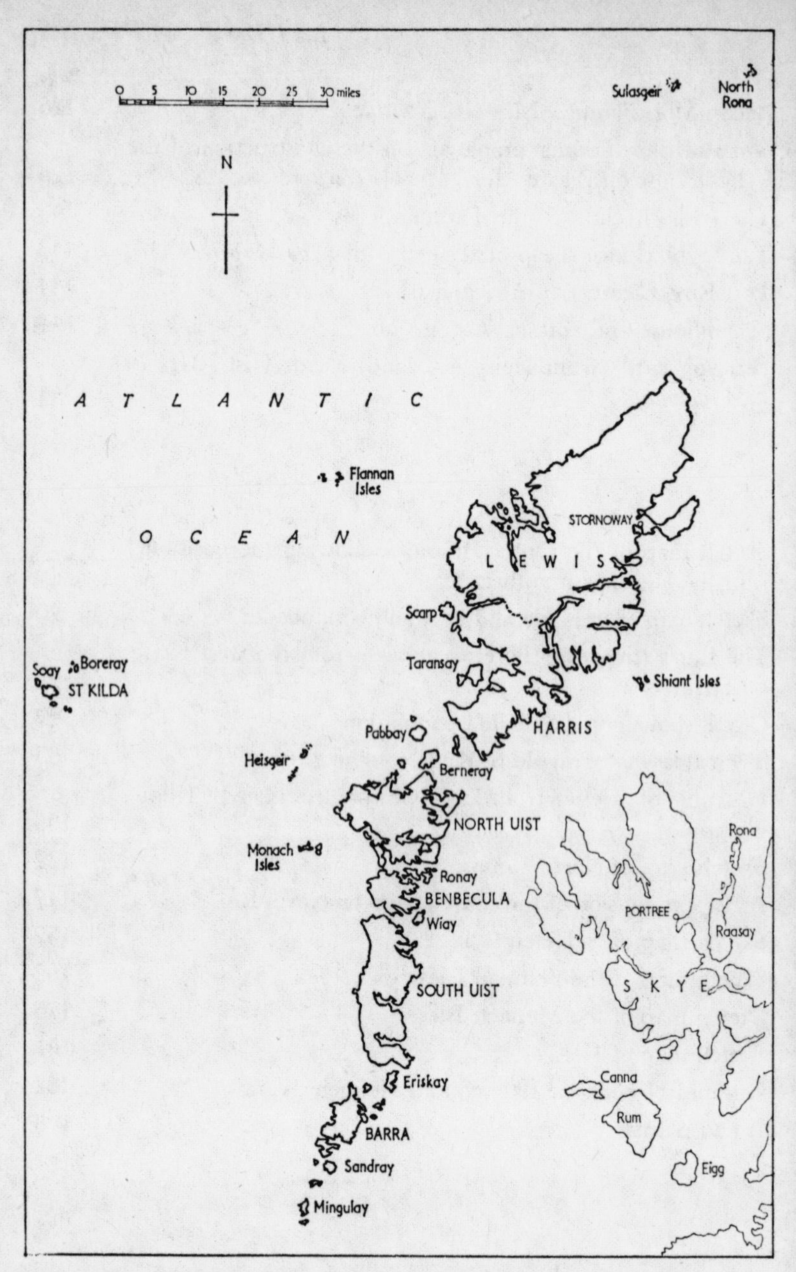

Sketch map of the Outer Hebrides, showing the positions of the Hebridean outliers

INTRODUCTION

ISLANDS form both a particular and a peculiar element in the topography of Scotland. Though an accurate total has never been arrived at, it is estimated that there are some 790 islands, of which under 200 have ever been inhabited. Today only about fifty are populated.

In the eighteenth century, some eight per cent of Scots lived on islands. Today the figure is less than two per cent. Even so, the population living on islands in the Highlands and Islands region is some thirty per cent (about 90,000) of the total Highlands population. Thus island-living is still significant to many people in Scotland today.

Most of Scotland's islands are found in her three archipelago-groups: Orkney, Shetland and the Hebrides. Of these, perhaps only the latter has witnessed a rich and full course of history from ancient times to the present day. During the last two centuries, the Hebridean islands have seen considerable social changes, and declined as an area of importance to the Scottish nation as a whole.

Today, Scotland's islands, both large and small, are faced with many problems: serious depopulation through migration; the highest rate of unemployment in Britain; and an unfair remoteness aspect imposed on them because the central government has concentrated an inordinate proportion of the nation's resources on developing areas with dense urban populations rather than those areas which still support essentially rural societies. The islands of Scotland are an exceptional problem within the British Isles. In particular, the populations on the presently-inhabited islands live at a low level compared with the degree of social well-being accepted by the rest of the country.

It was in 1861 that a census report first offered a definition of an island. 'An island,' it stated, 'is any piece of solid land surrounded by water, which affords sufficient vegetation to support one or more sheep, or which is inhabited by man.' This definition excluded 'all mere rocks which are the resort of wild fowl', unless the same were of sufficient extent to afford pasture to one or more sheep, when they were considered as islands. The 1861 census also said: 'Some of the uninhabited islands are of great extent and afford pasturage to from 300 to 400 sheep, and others again are very small—so small as only to admit of one sheep being left there at once, which is removed when fattened, and its place supplied by a leaner member of the flock.'

The islands which are the subject of this book were, with two exceptions, populated at one time in their history; some until as recently as thirty years ago. With the exception of Sulasgeir and the Flannans, men have found them eminently acceptable places on which to establish themselves, their homes, and their families, and to build up a community. They gave opportunity for a fulfilment of life which is denied the urban or even the rural dweller. They are, for the most part, sub-oceanic islands, placed deep in the Atlantic, yet reasonably accessible to the mainland of the nearest island-mass. Three of the islands, and island-groups, are, even today, capable of supporting small yet numerically and socially significant populations which could be largely self-supporting economically by reason of the natural resources of either the land itself or the surrounding seas. Given the necessary communication—and therefore social—links, these islands could become a homeplace again.

The islands were chosen for three reasons: first because they lie, for the most part, outside the main associated Hebridean group; secondly because, as Hebridean outliers, they display particular characteristics relevant to wild life today; and thirdly because their story is that of many other larger islands around the Scottish coast which have become depopulated.

An analysis of the factors leading to the ultimate desertion of an island by its population will reveal a number of reasons, social, economic and psychological.

From the social viewpoint it can be argued that the provision of adequate social services is as much a right of an island community as it is of an urban one. But in many ways island-living causes conflict in remote centres of administration among those who must on the one hand satisfy the dictates of an economically-oriented society through its elected government and, on the other hand, the wishes of a community which elects to remain in old, well-tried and well-established environments. In addition there is, particularly in the economically minded governments of our industrialised and urbanised society, the attitude that island populations do not contribute anything real to the nation's economic and social well-being. In fact, it is generally considered that people who take it on themselves to live on islands, remote from civilisation, have to make their own living as best they can and not look to other taxpayers' money to subsidise their 'escapism'. While the economist may have the last say, particularly in Britain, in other countries the decision of the political economist is tempered with a realisation that social and moral obligations are part and parcel of government and that the wishes of remote island communities must be respected.

From a psychological point of view, the failure of Scotland's island population to maintain its numbers (163,000 in 1861; 90,000 in 1961) and to develop the resources of its islands and the seas around them can be attributed largely to the control of a remote administrative centre. In other parts of the world, as in the Faroes, similar island groups have been offered and granted independence, or at least such a strong measure of devolution that the islands can work out their own salvation with only themselves to account to for any subsequent failure. Devolution or a measure of self-determination is necessary for an island-group to establish an identity to which the islanders can owe their primary allegiance. Failure to identify oneself as part of a definite pattern leads to an inferiority complex which, sooner or later, results in an effort to disassociate oneself physically by emigration from the image imposed by central government.

Remoteness, often given as the main factor in island depopulation, is an artificial one. Methods of transport are available today which bring remote areas in Canada very close to the larger centres of population. That the helicopter is ignored while ships are still used in dangerous waters to give islands reasonable communication links is evidence that the political administrator has hardly considered the potential viability of islands in this country.

His counterpart in many European and Scandinavian countries has played a much more significant role in the maintenance and enhancement of island communities. Smallness of an island is sometimes said to be the ultimate reason for depopulation. Yet there are large islands in the Hebridean, Shetland and Orkney groups which are suffering from depopulation at an alarming rate which, if continued, will mean their complete desertion by the end of this century. It is in the end the nation which stands to lose from this process which obliterates the deep-down burning desire of islanders to keep and care for their islands for coming generations.

Of the islands in this book perhaps St Kilda best tells the message for those island communities who, in response to a deep-inborn instinct, are opposed to the desertion of their island homes. Roland Svensson, author of *Lonely Isles* has this to say:

> The assistance given to outlying islands and isolated communities should be far bigger and more far-sighted. Take Britain for example. The population rises yearly. The need for arable land, canning factories, freezing plants and fishing vessels will be of paramount importance. People ask: 'who will pay?' Well, I will give you a drastic example. Look at St Kilda, lying about fifty miles west of the Outer Hebrides. The people were evacuated in 1930, partly because they were unable to maintain communications with the mainland. About eight years ago (in 1957) I saw the Forces move into that island. They brought bulldozers, tractors, big lorries, diesel generators, helicopters and so on, and regular communications were established with the mainland. But if an island woman of Foula in Shetland, or Fair Isle, or Canna in the Inner Hebrides is to give birth to a child, there will be no helicopter to bring her to a mainland hospital. Who paid for all these wonderful modern implements, tractors and lorries? The British paid for them. And we ought to be able to invest the far smaller sum necessary to assist island populations, building what would be of lasting importance.

Today, in Scotland, more than one hundred islands, once inhabited, stand deserted. Their desertion, however, has not meant that they have become derelict, useless hulks lying like anchored flotsam in the fertile ocean. They still retain much of their inherent potential. Many islands have played an increasingly significant agricultural role subsequent to their depopulation. They offer valuable pasturage which can be improved without the problem of over-grazing which rendered them marginal when they were inhabited. Although of course fewer persons stand to benefit from this cycle of desertion and pastoral re-colonisation, they still make an important contribution to the income of the owner or tenant. Deserted islands offer additional advantages: for livestock, they provide ideal escape-proof pens and folds, protected from disturbance and disease, with their mild maritime climate allowing out-wintering. These factors considered, islands can, and often do, make a significant contribution to the crofting economy as it is developing in the Highlands and Islands today. It may well be that our deserted islands, however unsuited they are for present day settlement, could offer an invaluable increment to the national store of productive land in an age when farming land is being swallowed up by sites for industry and housing.

It is of course when people are considered that the emotive word 'tragedy' tends to intrude in a final assessment of Scotland's islands and their future. This human aspect of the island problem is of particular interest to the sociologist. Desertion is often interpreted as man's failure to grapple with the hostile environment of the island. This an over-simplification. An anlysis of contemporary trends in island depopulation in other parts of the world reveals that, rather than simple failure, desertion reflects a balancing up of population with basic resources in the light of new opportunities and accelerated by the desire to maintain a reasonable degree of social participation with nearby large communities. It is often the very small islands—supporting only a family or two—which are deserted first. Isolation rather than insularity is often the main cause of desertion: this is as evident in the Outer Hebrides, in Orkney or the Shetland Islands as it is in islands in other parts of the world.

Even so, islands still offer a special kind of environment, appealing to people who are willing to work hard for the rewards which come from a basic desire to mark out their own lives. Far from being society drop-outs, there are many who prefer the opportunities for personal fulfilment which only an island environment can offer. Electing, as they do, to keep far corners of a nation's land store alive, rather than let them revert to nature, island communities play a special role in their country's social and economic welfare.

Page 17: *(above)* St Kilda c 1890 showing the village; *(below)* general view of St Kilda as it is at present. Far background: village street; centre foreground: the church and manse (white house); extreme left: the ruins of 'The Store' used to contain the wool and tweeds awaiting collection by the steamer. The old cannon can be seen at the gable end of the ruin.

Page 18: *(above)* Families outside the houses in Main Street, St Kilda c 1890; *(below)* dividing the catch of fulmars on St Kilda c 1890

1 ST KILDA: ISLAND AND SOCIETY

THE ISLANDS

General Description

THE island group of St Kilda lies about 34 miles WNW of the western extreme of North Uist in the Hebrides. The latitude is 57° 49′; longitude is 8° 34′. The group consists of three main islands: St Kilda or Hirt, Soay, and Boreray; together with an islet, Dun, lying close off St Kilda. There are three large and almost inaccessible rocks: Stac Levenish, Stac Lee and Stac an Armin.

Rising sheer out of the sea, when viewed from the Uist shore, the islands appear as great dull-coloured pillars on the horizon. Conachair on St Kilda rises skywards as the highest and most awe-inspiring cliff in the British Isles. Being completely exposed to the Atlantic Ocean the islands show in their configuration what wind, rain, sea and storm have worked during the passage of countless milleniums. What must have been gentle sloping coastlines are now steep, sheer cliff-faces, eroded and honeycombed with large caves, many of which extend for over 300 ft underground.

St Kilda, also known as Hirt, is 1,575 acres in extent and reaches its peak at the summit of Conachair (1,397 ft). Soay island extends to 244 acres, and is 1,225 ft at its highest point. The figures for the other masses in the group are: Boreray, 189 acres, 1,245 ft at the summit; Dun, 79 acres, 576 ft high; Stac an Armin, 13 acres, 627 ft high; Stac Levenish, 6 acres, 185 ft high; and Stac Lee, 6 acres, 544 ft high.

The islands are formed of tertiary igneous rocks which display suggestions of glacial erosion. These volcanic rocks are estimated to be the same age as those of the volcanic series found in the Inner Hebrides: Skye, Rhum, Mull and Ardnamurchan. John MacCulloch, the nineteenth-century geologist who thoroughly investigated the islands, indicated specifically gabbro and granite.

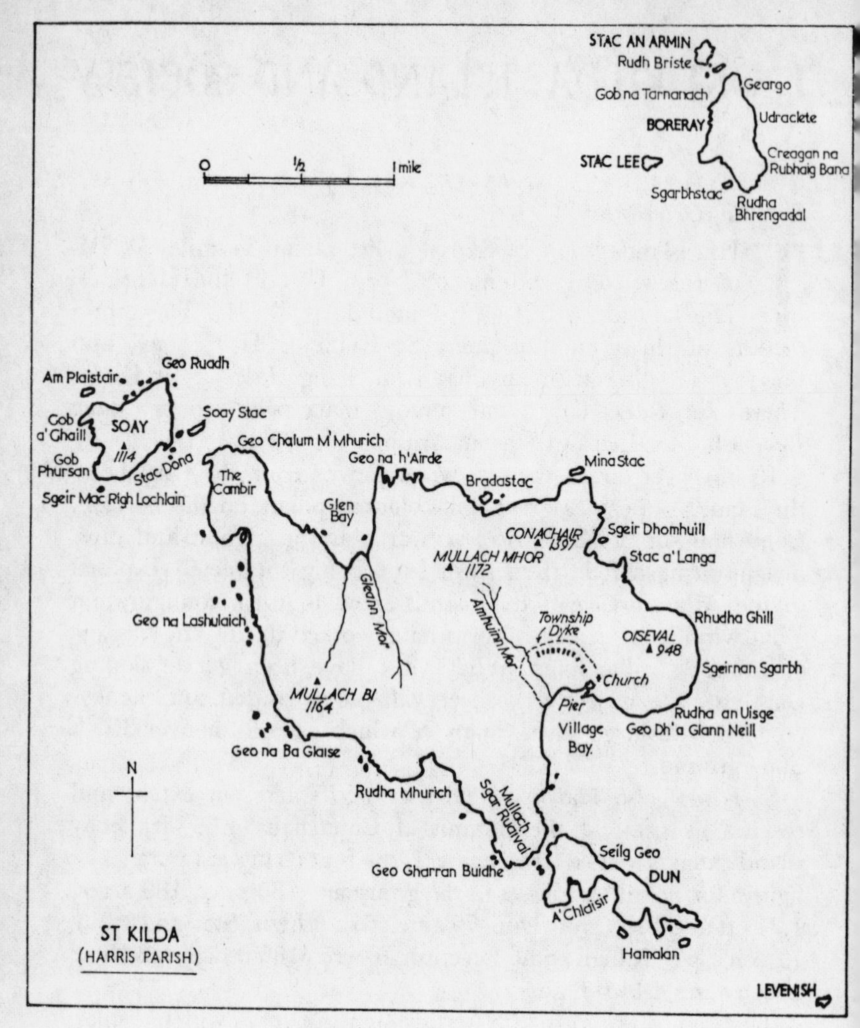

Sketch map of St Kilda and its satellite islands

The granite was the first rock to be erupted; this was followed by the gabbros in the third stage of volcanic activity of the tertiary period. Thus the basic rocks of the island group are: gabbros, composed of diallage, plagioclase felspar, olivine, and magnetite; dolerites; and basalts. The eastern part of St Kilda island is chiefly granite and of a light colour. The dark crags and eroded pinnacles of other parts of the main island, and of the other islands and islets, are of gabbro. Some of the St Kilda rock is strongly magnetic.

St Kilda, Dun, Stac Levenish

St Kilda, the largest island of the group, is approached for landing purposes only from the western or eastern sides. On the western side is Glen Bay, whose landward parts at some time in the island's obscure history supported a settlement which was later supposedly abandoned for the eastern Village Bay where the present, now-deserted, settlement still remains. Though an occasional landing can be made at some of the island's caves, the risks are often too great for this to be done at any other time but in an emergency. Approaching St Kilda from the eastern side, into Village Bay, one immediately becomes aware of the stage-like appearance of this the island's second settlement. Like an amphitheatre, the semi-circular bay has on each side steep and fast-rising slopes. At low water, a good sandy beach is exposed which gives way to some shelving rocks and a storm beach. Above this, the grassy ground runs up to the village and beyond.

The two hills which overlook the bay are Oseval and Conachair. They are of cream-coloured granite, weathered into rough blocks which have, in another time, rolled down to the sea margin, forming a rough talus in the crevices of which grows a coarse vegetation. This forms the arable land. The soil supports a good turf and it has been suggested that had it been allowed to evolve, instead of being continually skimmed by generations of islanders for fuel, it would have been extremely useful agricultural land able to yield a wide variety of produce. The hills are grassy to their summits. A conspicuous gully, containing a stream, runs down the western side of Conachair. Glen Bay is a smaller indentation, from the head of which a straight valley runs south-eastward between the hills; there is a stream which falls into the bay waters. Apart from the two bays, the coastline of St Kilda is extremely rugged.

With his accustomed eloquence, Geikie described Conachair:

> Nowhere among the Inner Hebrides, not even on the south-western side of Rum, is there any such display of the capacity of the youngest granite to assume the most rugged and picturesque forms. It is hardly possible to exaggerate the variety of outline assumed by the rock as it yields along its system of joints to the influence of a tempestuous climate. It has been carved into huge projecting buttresses and deep alcoves, the naked stone glowing with tints of orange and fawn colour, veiled here and there with patches of bright green slope, or edged with fringes of sea-pink and camomile. Every outstanding bastion is rent with chasms and split into blocks, which accumulate on the ledges like piles of ruined walls. To one who boats underneath these cliffs the scene of ceaseless destruction which they present is vividly impressive.

The islet of Dun is a remarkable rocky ridge which at one time was connected to St Kilda, but is now separated by a narrow, rock-strewn channel. It lies off the south-eastern end of St Kilda. The ridge is precipitous on both sides. The contour of Bioda Mor, the highest peak, is serrated in a fantastic manner. The south-western coast is much indented while the north-eastern side is steep, green and grassy. Dun is penetrated by a natural tunnel, through which the sea flows. Though the islet is separated from St Kilda only by 100 yd or so, landing is extremely difficult and requires a smooth sea. A slithery crossing can be effected at very low tides. Dun is about 1 mile long and varies in width from 100–200 ft.

Stac Levenish lies 1 mile to the east of Dun and is a high rock in the shape of a pyramid.

Boreray, Stac Lee, Stac an Armin

Boreray lies some 3½ miles NE of St Kilda. It is an island of precipices and is the most difficult to land on, even in good weather. The coast-line consists of high, black cliffs, many of them rising into curious peaks from 300–1,000 ft high. On the east side of the island there is a grassy slope of some 40° steepness; the west side is sheer cliff. Landing is effective only near the southern end of the island close to Sgarbhstac, a low-lying, sea-washed rock.

Boreray is important for an unusual reason. Recent investigations, carried out on the megalithic sites in Britain to discover the reasons for their origins, have resulted in a strong theory that the island's summit was used as a calendar marker in association with menhirs erected *c* BC 1790 on the Outer Hebrides. These stand-

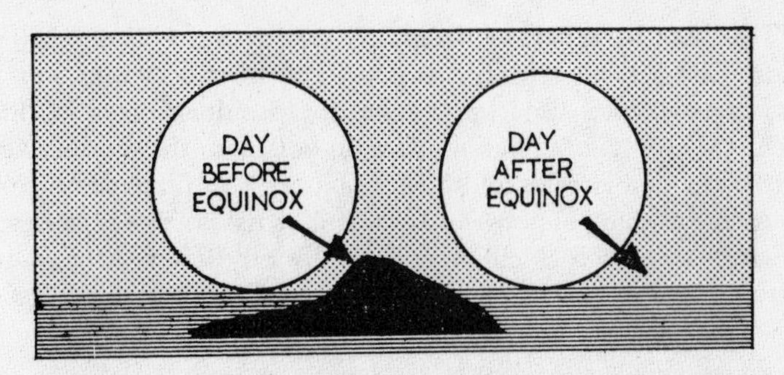

The sun setting over Boreray as seen from the west coast of Harris. The large monolith, Clach Mhic Leoid (MacLeod's Stone), points out to Boreray, and is so aligned that the autumn equinox can be calculated. Three other stones on the Harris coast use Boreray as a sighting point. On the day of the equinox, the sun sets directly behind the summit of the island

ing stones are An Carra, on South Uist; an oriented stone on Benbecula; Clach an t-Sagairt, on North Uist; and Clach Mhic-Leoid, on Harris. With the sun setting behind Boreray, all these stones give primary calendar declinations. The last three stone slabs are all oriented on Boreray with an accuracy that can only be described as deliberate. The island summit was used as an accurate foresight to give the same date in the evening as the sun set.

Lying close to Boreray are Stac Lee and Stac an Armin. Stac Lee has been described by Sir Julian Huxley as 'the most majestic sea rock in existence'. It lies about 600 yd west of Boreray. It is a curious rock. Its long axis lies NW and SE and it is steeper at the ends than at the sides. Both ends overhang and it has been estimated that the height of the rock is double the least measurement across the base.

Stac an Armin lies about 300 yd off Boreray's north-west face. Rising to over 600 ft it offers, as does its sister stac, a home for nesting gannets. It has been estimated that about one-quarter of the world's gannet stock nests on these two stacks or on neighbouring Boreray.

Soay

This island is separated from St Kilda by a strait some 500 yd wide. Cliff-girt all round, it is flattish on top and wears a green turf cap which is used for grazing the primitive breed of Soay sheep. The only safe landing place on Soay is at the south-eastern end. Stac na Biorrach and Stac Dona are two pinnacles of rock lying in the channel between Soay and St Kilda. The former was the subject of a rock-climb in 1698 by Sir Robert Moray. His subsequent description of the venture is said to be the earliest of any climb in Britain.

> . . . After they landed, a man having room but for one of his feet, he must climb up 12 or 16 fathoms high. Then he comes to a place where, having but room for his left foot and left hand, he must leap from thence to another place before him, which if he hit right the rest of the ascent is easie, and with a small cord which he carries with him he hales up a rope whereby all the rest come up. But if he misseth that footstep (as often times they do) he falls into the sea, and the company takes him in by the small cord and he sits still until he is a little refreshed and then he tries it again; for everyone there is not able for that sport.

The Present Day

The whole St Kilda group is in the care and keeping of the National Trust for Scotland and is leased to the Nature Conservancy. The Trust annually organises working parties which endeavour to maintain the more important buildings in a reasonable state of preservation; in this respect St Kilda is an interesting social museum. Cottages, cleits and other structures are kept in good repair so that visitors can taste at least some of the atmosphere of St Kilda as it was before the evacuation of 1930. The Trust also runs big-ship cruises which take in all the Hebridean outliers and the main islands in the Outer and Inner Hebridean chain. Landings are made on St Kilda, when the weather permits, though the cruise-parties must content themselves with close-up views of Sulasgeir, North Rona, and the Flannans.

The Nature Conservancy is at present engaged in carrying out an ecological survey on St Kilda. The results of this will be more than interesting in that it will assess the extent of the changes brought about by some four decades of man's disappearance from the island.

In 1957, the government announced the acquisition of an area in South Uist in the Hebrides for a rocket-firing base. A small section of Hirt, the main island in the St Kilda group, is now leased to the Ministry of Defence to accommodate the military personnel together with a few Hebridean civilians employed in tracking guided-missiles fired from South Uist.

In 1969, some £500,000 was spent in lengthening the pier in Village Bay and in erecting new buildings at the military camp. The camp site has electricity and cinemas, living quarters with efficient heating systems, a signals centre, radar station, offices, workshops, stores, an oil installation and a small power station. There is helicopter communication with the Scottish mainland.

Perhaps as an indication of how St Kilda is part of the present, one might mention that in 1969 the BBC, for the first time in its history, had a request for a Gaelic song from St Kilda, from some Uistmen who were working on the building of the new pier.

St Kilda is a sad monument to one of the world's small human tragedies, in which man and not nature played the leading role. At the time of the evacuation MacLeod of MacLeod received over 400 requests from people who wanted to take up where the islanders left off, but they were refused permission. At the present there are signs that islands in general are being regarded as useful bases on which to found new communities and we may well see St Kilda with a non-military resident population again.

THE ISLANDERS

Island Society

The St Kildan society was one in whose evolutionary process remoteness played an important part. The result, however, was not a true sub-species of *homo sapiens* for the reason that the island society was latterly not wholly the same as that which had existed on the island some two thousand years ago. Island tradition indicates that on at least two possible occasions during its early history the society was all but obliterated : once during the changeover (if this did take place at all) from the settlement in Gleann Mor to that in Village Bay; and, secondly, when two St Kilda men, Duigan and Fearchar, committed all their fellow islanders to the flames inside the island's church—all save the old woman survivor who escaped to tell the tale.

Nor, from Martin's time (1697) to the island's evacuation (1930) can the St Kildan society be said to be a complete survival or take-over from the earliest centuries. In many ways, the manner in which the island society organised itself and created its own environment was similar to that of the communities on the nearby Hebrides. Because the island society was, however, effectively insulated from many of the wider external sophisticating influences, it retained certain aspects which were peculiar to St Kilda and to nowhere else.

Population

The highest population recorded on the island was 180 in 1697, when Martin Martin visited the island. When the island was evacuated in 1930, 36 people left the shores of Village Bay. At various times from the year of Martin's visit the population figures were recorded and show, over a period of about 230 years, a gradual decline. The population curve shows both erratic fluctuations (smallpox and cholera epidemics, and the 1856 migration when 36 people left the island) and small increases (the slight increases of births over deaths and the small additive immigrant stock settling on the island).

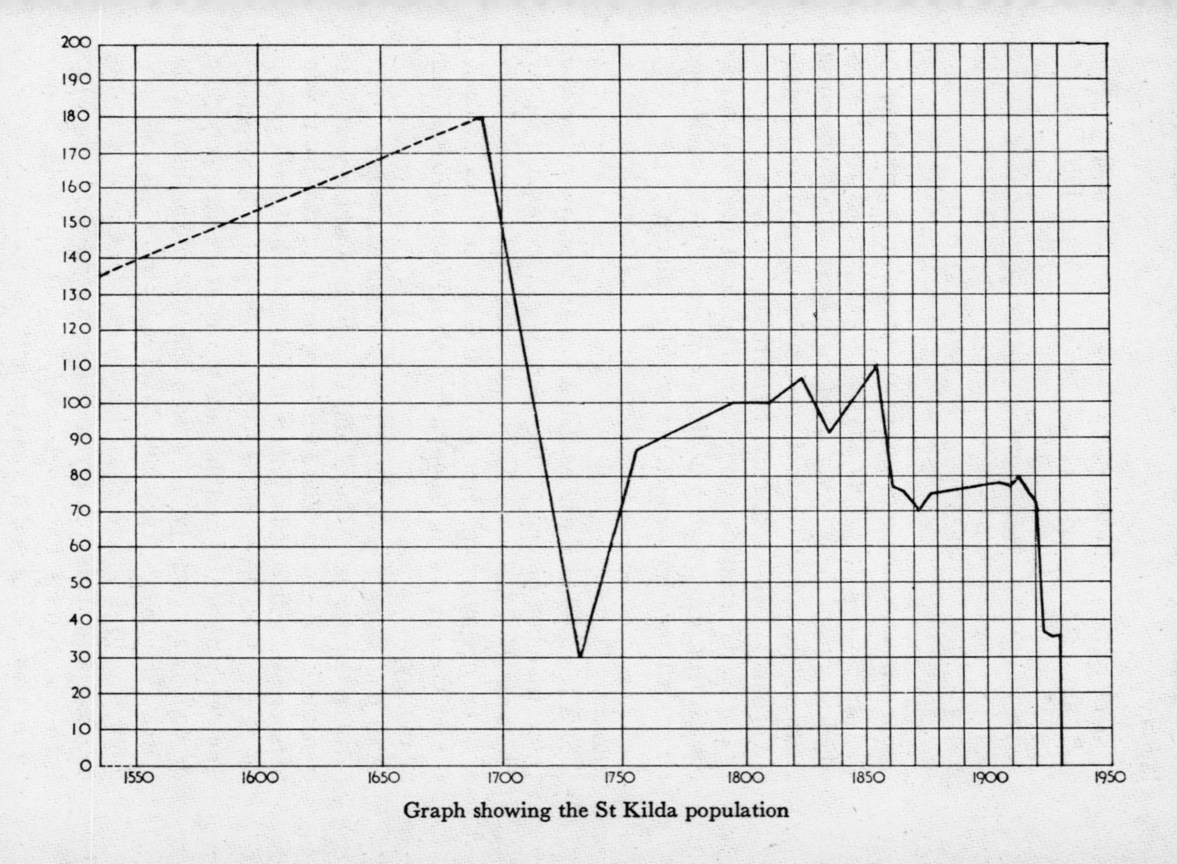

Graph showing the St Kilda population

The following figures show the decline in the St Kildan population:

1697	180	1838	92	1884	77	1928	37
1730	30	1851	110	1906	78	1930	36
1758	88	1861	78	1910	77		
1799	100	1866	77	1911	80		
1810	*c*100	1871	71	1920	73		
1822	108	1877	76	1921	73		

The smallpox epidemic in 1730 reduced the population to thirty people and the community had to be restocked from Harris, whence many of the later surnames might have come. Subsequent intermarriage probably erased any characteristics in the indigenous population which had survived till then.

The sex differentiation, so far as can be ascertained, was largely non-existent, except when a disaster at sea, *c* 1865, caused the loss of eight men and resulted in a sexual imbalance.

Ancestry

St Kildan tradition tells us that it was an Irish rover, one Mac Quin, who first landed on the main island to found a colony. The surname MacQueen has always been popular in St Kilda, as in the neighbouring island of North Uist. The name in Gaelic is Mac Chuinn (son of Conn) a figure who looms large in Irish mythology.

Another island legend has it that St Kilda was won in a race between the people of Harris and Uist, both of whom wanted to own the island group. The factions agreed that two boats were to be crewed with equal numbers of men and whichever crew was the first to lay a hand on St Kilda would own it in perpetuity. The two boats set off and the race proved to be extremely close. As both boats came hard by St Kilda, one of the men in the Harris (MacLeod) crew, Colla MacLeod, cut off his hand and threw it onto the shore, thus cheating the Uist crew of an undoubted prize. This deed is recorded by a red hand in the MacLeod coat of arms. One might compare this story with the race for the possession of North Rona (page 127).

Tradition also refers to the 'first MacDonald'. He is supposed to be Archibald (Gillespie) Dhu, who murdered his two legitimate brothers about 1506. Gregory, in his *History of Scotland*, says that this man joined a band of pirates and, while he harboured on St Kilda, founded a family there. This story, however, is not borne out by other traditions, one of which indicates that the St Kilda MacDonalds claimed kinship with Clanranald of South Uist.

The two clans which can claim to be the oldest on the island are, firstly, Mac Ille Mhoirre (Mac Ghille Mhuire = son of the servant of Mary), rendered Morison, a family of Norse descent of whom there is a great concentration in the north of Lewis; and, secondly, Mac Ille Rhiabhich, the translation of which appears to be 'son of the grizzly man'. The etymology of this surname has defied investigation but might well refer to Norse Berserks warriors, or to the furs with which the Norsemen were clothed during their ascendancy in the Western Isles. Thus, one might say that the St Kildan of modern times is of Norse/Celtic descent, with the strains intermingled.

The St Kildan surnames such as MacLeod and MacCrimmon were obvious imports from the Hebrides, Skye and elsewhere. In 1843, the order of surnames on St Kilda was MacDonald (most numerous), MacLeod, Gillies, Morison, MacQueen, MacKinnon and MacCrimmon. In 1871, the order had changed: Gillies, MacDonald, Ferguson, MacKinnon, MacCrimmon, MacQueen and MacKay (the last two were the minister and the registrar). It will be noticed that two former families, MacLeods and Morisons, are not mentioned, they having either died out or emigrated. About 1889, the MacCrimmons had also gone.

Characteristics

From descriptions of the appearance of St Kildans over the centuries, the islanders seem to have been well-built with definite Norse characteristics: '. . . they had rather long aquiline and pensive cast of feature, with well-marked eyebrows. They are well made and about middle size'.

Inevitably the islanders were simple when they were confronted with sophisticates. An anecdote is told of the islanders' inability to think deeply to assess the implications of much of what they were taught. At one time the Rev Neil MacKenzie (minister from 1830–44) told the St Kildans of the other races in the world. They were particularly interested in the South Sea Islanders with whom they found a kinship. Shortly afterwards, a number of shipwrecked men were found by the St Kildans in a cave. They hailed them both in English and Gaelic but failed to get any response from the crew. The minister was informed that a new race had landed on the island, probably South Sea Islanders. In fact, the crew were from the wrecked *Hispania* and responded to the minster's 'Quae gens'.

On another occasion, a visiting boat had no sooner left the island when a storm broke and the vessel was in danger of drifting onto the island's sharp rocks. To a man, the St Kildans left their firesides and went to the church where they prayed steadfastly for several hours until, perhaps by a miracle, the wind changed and the ship was able to make for the safety of Village Bay. This charity of the islanders shines above their natural simplicity which so many visitors took merely, and shallowly, as something extraordinary to write home about.

That the islanders were hospitable to all visitors is related in many records. Their moral character has always been high, probably the result of the self-policing aspects which small communities often exhibit. Swearing and theft were unknown in St Kilda when Martin Martin went there in 1697. In 1758, when the Rev MacAulay stayed in St Kilda, he found the people simple, hospitable, polite and untainted with vice. He saw no cases of drunkenness, though he did observe that the men were overfond of tobacco. The first illegitimate birth on the island occurred in 1862; after that only two other cases were recorded.

Martin Martin quotes an amusing account of a visit to Glasgow by a St Kildan:

> He was astonished at the length of the voyage, and of the great kingdoms, as he thought them, that is isles, by which they sailed; the largest in his way did not exceed twenty-four miles in length, but he considered how much they exceed his own little native country. Upon his arrival at Glasgow, he was like one that had dropped from the clouds into a new world, whose language, habits &c., were in all respects new to him; he never

imagined that such big houses of stone were made with hands; and for the pavements of the streets, he thought it must needs be altogether natural, for he could not believe that men would be at the pains to beat stones into the ground to walk upon. He stood dumb at the door of his lodging, with the greatest admiration; and when he saw a coach and two horses, he thought it to be a little house they were drawing at their tail, with men in it; but he condemned the coachman for a fool to sit so uneasy, for he thought it safer to sit on the horse's back. The mechanism of the coach-wheel, and its running about, was the greatest of all his wonders. When he went through the streets, he desired to have one to lead him by the hand. Thomas Ross, a merchant, and others, that took the diversion to carry him through the town, asked his opinion of the High Church? He answered that it was a large rock, yet there were some in St Kilda much higher, but that these were the best caves he ever saw; for that was the idea which he conceived of the pillars and arches upon which the church stands. When they carried him into the church, he was yet more surprised, and held up his hands with admiration, wondering how it was possible for men to build such a prodigious fabric, which he supposed to be the largest in the universe. He could not imagine what the pews were designed for, and he fancied the people that wore masks (not knowing whether they were men or women) had been guilty of some ill things for which they dared not show their faces. He was amazed at women wearing patches, and fancied them to have been blisters. Pendants seemed to him the most ridiculous of all things; he condemned periwigs mightily, and much more the powder used in them; in fine, he condemned all things as superfluous he saw not in his own country. He looked with amazement on everything that was new to him. When he heard the church-bells ring, he was under a mighty consternation, as if the fabric of the world had been in great disorder. He did not think there had been so many people in the world as in the City of Glasgow; and it was a great mystery to him to think what they could all design by living so many in one place . . . when he saw big loaves, he could not tell whether they were bread, stone or wood. He was amazed to think how they could be provided with ale, for he never saw any there that drank water. He wondered how they made them fine clothes, and to see stockings made without first being cut, and afterwards sewn, was no small wonder to him. He thought it foolish in women to wear thin silks, as being a very improper habit for such as pretended to any sort of employment. When he saw the women's feet, he judged them to be of another shape than those of the men, because of the different shape of their shoes. He did not approve of the heels of shoes worn by men or women; and when he observed horses with shoes on their feet, and fastened with iron nails, he could not forbear laughing, and thought it the most ridiculous thing that ever fell under his observation. He longed to see his native country again, and passionately wished it were blessed with ale, brandy, tobacco, and iron, as Glasgow was.

Speech

Being strengthened by immigrants at intervals during the life of the community, and particularly after the smallpox epidemic in 1724, the vocabulary of the St Kildan's native language, Gaelic, showed very few peculiarities. About 1843, the minister on the island noted that the only linguistic differences were in the shades of meaning which the islanders attached to a few words. There were occasional differences in the manner in which they pronounced words in which 'r' occurred; this consonant they pronounced as 'l' (eg *ruith* = to run, was *luith*). This may well have been an importation from some of the Hebridean islands. MacAulay (1758) reported that the St Kildans had a very corrupt dialect of Gaelic, with a slight admixture of Norse, whilst every native islander had an incorrigible lisp. The increased intercourse with the Hebrides probably improved the islanders' Gaelic but failed to eradicate their lisp, which was also noted in 1843.

Houses and Store-houses

All that the original settlers of St Kilda considered necessary was supplied by their own island, together with the facilities offered by Soay and Boreray, and the intermittent communications link with the Hebridean islands to the east. In many respects, the St Kildan community was more fortunate in its environment than was the sister community of North Rona. The island of St Kilda or Hirt was large, though perhaps awkward in that much of it was sloping ground. It had, however, two fertile glens, fresh water in many wells and springs, and there were two suitable landing places, each of which could be chosen according to the prevailing weather and sea conditions.

The first accommodation provided was in the form most commonly found in the Hebrides: subterranean dwellings or hypogea. These afforded the necessary warmth in the winter seasons.

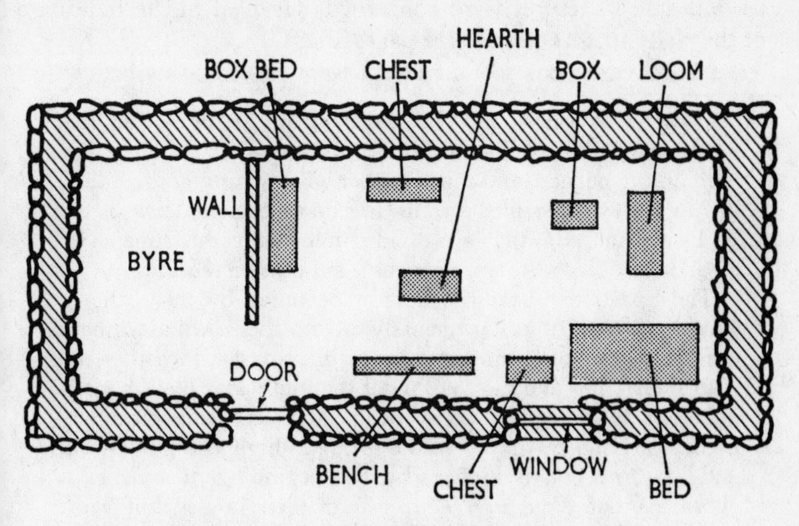

Typical layout of an old St Kilda cottage c 1850

They consisted of stone-walled pits with compartments. The settlement in Gleann Mor is largely composed of this type of structure. In the course of time, the walls were increased in height to rise proud of the ground and the structures took the shape of the familiar 'black house'.

By 1697, the year of Martin Martin's visit to the island, the 'black house' structure was well in evidence, with a timber roof thatched with straw, 'the whole secured by ropes of twisted Heath, the Extremity of which on each side is poised with Stone to preserve the Thatch from being blown away'. This use of a wooden ridge-pole and couples permitted a roomier house, for in the earlier type, with a ceiling of slabs, the breadth had been severely limited by the builder's skill in corbelling the walls. Some structures, which had obviously been hovels in the mid seventeenth century, had had their gables lifted by additional granite blocks arranged to take a long timber, perhaps a storm-blown tree-trunk washed up on the beach, which then supported a thatched roof.

The corbelling technique, though it became archaic insofar as domestic structures were concerned, survived in the building of the cleits or store-houses (see pages 37–8).

In 1838, the houses of St Kilda were described as being:

> constructed of rough stones built without any art, or mortar, save a little earth. The walls are from 5 to 8 feet thick, about 5 feet high on the outside, and much higher when empty in the inside, having no windows in the walls, nor doors but one towards the N. East. Internally they are divided into two compartments by a partition of loose stones, removable as occasion requires.
>
> The apartment next the door is occupied by the cattle in winter, and the other by themselves. Into their own apartment they begin early in summer to gather peat-dust, which they use with their ashes and moisten by all the foul water used in making their food, &c. By these means, the floor rises gradually higher and higher, till it is in the spring as high as the side-wall, and in some houses higher. By the beginning of summer a person cannot stand *upright* in any of their houses, but, *must creep on all fours round the fire*.

Another early nineteenth-century description is contained in the Notes of the Rev MacKenzie:

> Of their most ancient houses several still remain entire. They are circular, or nearly so, and roughly built. The walls are 6 or 7 feet thick, with spaces for beds left in them. These bed spaces are roofed with long slabs, and the entrance from the interior of the house is about 3 feet by 2 feet. The walls are not arched but contracted gradually by the overlapping of the stones to nearly a point. The entrance door is about 3 feet by 2½. The outside is covered with earth and rubbish and appears like a green hillock. In some places they are almost entirely underground . . . The only opening for light was a small circular opening at one end where the thatch joined the wall,

Page 35: *(above)* Islanders at the pier on the day before evacuation of St Kilda; *(below)* Island tourists wave a fond farewell to St Kilda

Page 36: St Kilda: *(above)* the cliffs of Boreray; *(below)* the island today showing new buildings and, in the background, the gap between the main island Hirt and Dun

left for the exit of the smoke. The door aperture was near the end and faced the east.

These houses were built in two rows, abundantly regular and facing one another, with a tolerable causeway in the middle, which they call the Street.

Soon after the date of this description, the settlement in Village Bay moved farther east to the site of the present housing area. The move was instigated by the Rev MacKenzie himself. An Englishman, Sir Thomas Ackland, provided a financial incentive. From 1836–8 twenty-five houses, barns and outbuildings were built. The style of construction was similar to that found in the Outer Hebrides: double-thickness walls with earth packed tight between them. The roof ended at the inner wall and was shaped like a large beehive. It was made of wood and was covered first with turf and then thatched with straw. Thick ropes, made from straw, were stretched across the thatch and were secured with the beaks of gannets. These improved houses had a sort of window with a tiny piece of glass in it. Wooden locks, of native make, secured the doors. Both the window and lock were innovations for the island. The fire remained in the middle of the floor, where it had been for centuries.

The furnishings of the St Kildan dwellings were always simple. In the mediaeval houses there was a quern, a hollow stone called a *clach soluis* filled with oil and a cinder of peat for a wick the whole to serve as a lamp, a vessel called a *cragan* made of badly burnt clay and used for a pot, a water pitcher and a dish to drink out of, a rope made of hide, and some stools. Later, the furniture included a couple of iron pots, a chest or two, wooden dishes, straw baskets, an iron oil-filled lamp called a *cruisgean*, and stools. Extras included chairs, dressers, straw mattresses, kettles and wooden beds. But even in 1875, the minister was the only person on the island to possess a fork.

As the influence of tourists made itself felt, the furnishings in the island homes took on more contemporary aspects, though this did not bring with it an incentive to keep a tidy home. Through the centuries, reports invariably indicate the St Kildan's penchant for untidiness and domestic chaos.

The cleits, or store-houses, have often created much interest as they are literally scattered up the slopes of Conachair and stud the rising land like large boulders. The cleits show the survival of the building techniques used on the island many centuries ago. They are little stone-built cells with high crowned roofs covered with green turf and vegetation. In the wet climate of the island, the cleits were of vital importance to the community, as they offered storage for peat, nets used for fishing, hay, and the birds caught by the fowlers. Their drystone walls allowed the wind to seep through, ventilating the stores, while the turf roofs repelled the heavy rains.

Captain F. W. L. Thomas, the antiquarian who did so much to record the antiquities of the Hebrides during the last century, describes one cleit:

> Its dimensions inside are only 8 feet by 2½ feet by 5 feet; the enclosing wall is built purposely with wide joints, but the roof is covered with turf.

Mentioning that this was the construction of 'one of the rudest cleits', Thomas goes on to describe one of the larger structures:

> . . . it is 16 feet long, 6 feet broad, and 9 feet high internally. The door, not low, is at one end, and the other end is rounded. There was no window, but many *cuiltean* or niches in the walls, and it had been used as a dairy. The roof was formed by overlapping. Externally the walls were perpendicular and bare for 5 or 6 feet; they then fell in and were covered with turf. The aspect externally is that of an elongated pyramid with a green top; but had it been deserted, and the turf worn off, it would exactly resemble an old Irish oratory.

Clothing

In the environmental conditions which the island imposed, the islanders' dress was as functional as was their approach to hygiene and to living accommodation. In ancient times the inhabitants wore sheep skins, though this form of dress was not peculiar to St Kilda. In the nineteenth century they wore short jackets of their own make; trousers and waistcoats were also made in the home from the same rough cloth. The shoes were made from the necks of solan geese, cut from above the eyes. The crown served for the heel, with the down-side inwards. Others preferred the simple shoe of folded cow-hide, tanned and softened with native plants, and held on by a leather thong. Later in the nineteenth century the clothes of the St Kildans were little different from those worn in other parts of the Highlands and Islands. The men wore jackets, vests and trousers of their own making, mostly made from a coarse thick cloth called blue kelt. The men were also fond of wearing the Glengarry bonnet. The women's dresses were also home-made, from cloth made on the island and dyed with the juices of native plants. The women fancied the wearing of a plaid of Rob Roy tartan for Sundays; the plaid was fastened by a brooch. The weekday head-dress of the women was a turkey-red cotton napkin; on Sundays the older females wore the common white muslin cap or mutch. Many women and men went barefoot; the children always did so. With the influence of the tourists, stockings and boots became common. Personal ornaments were few among the islanders; most of those worn were made from copper or silver coins hammered into brooches and pins.

When John Sands visited the island in 1875 he found that:

> The St Kildans are warmly clothed, which probably accounts for the immunity they enjoy from pulmonary and other diseases. The men make all their own clothes, and also dresses for the women. The gowns of the latter seem of a very antique fashion. They are fastened on the breast with a large pin made from a ling hook. Their plaid is secured with a brooch made from an old penny. The bill of the sea-pyot or oyster catcher was formerly used as a pin for the gown and plaid. In warm weather the women are often to be seen on the cliffs and in the glen without any clothing but a woollen shirt. The men also strip to their underclothing when engaged on the cliffs. The *brog tiondadh*, or turned shoe, was universal until within a few years. Specimens are still to be seen. They are made without welts. Caps of lambskin were also the fashion, but I have only seen one. A live peat, stuck on the end of a stick, served for a lantern on a dark night. I have often used it myself.

SOCIAL ORGANISATION

The St Kildan social organisation was similar to that of that other island society, the North Rona community, in the matter of property, communal work and the preservation of discipline to prevent serious social disruption. Naturally, with the link which St Kilda had with the communities on the Hebrides and with Skye in particular, and as the community evolved from its primitive state, elements of sophistication appeared. Naturally, too, the community's organisation was based on the fact that St Kilda was a group of small land-masses surrounded by a hostile ocean.

MacLeod Ownership

For many centuries St Kilda was owned by the MacLeods of Harris and of Dunvegan in Skye. In general, the Chief of MacLeod was, through the centuries, fully aware of his social responsibility to the islanders. In a report, by Murray of Broughton, in connection with the social organisation of the Highlands and Islands in 1746 it was stated: 'Their Chief is their God, their everything.'

But the chief was not without reward for his concern and oversight—the island yielded a not insignificant source of economic return. A steward, usually nominated from a cadet branch of the MacLeod family, was placed in charge of the island. His deputy resided on St Kilda and had free lands, with special privileges among the islanders. The steward himself paid an annual visit to the island to collect the rents, which were paid in kind, the principal items being cloth, feathers, wool, butter, cheese, cows, horses, fowls, oil and barley. Any surplus in the island's production was taken by the steward to the Scottish mainland for sale and translation into the items which the islanders needed, particularly salt and seed corn. These he took with him to St Kilda on the following year's visit. This system was operated for centuries until it was no longer possible for the chief to accept rents in kind and a cash economy assumed importance in St Kilda.

Not all the stewards appointed by MacLeod were 'gentlemen of benevolent dispositions, of liberal education and much observation'. Some years before Martin's visit to the island in 1697, one steward attempted to extract a sheep from every family, but the islanders refused the demand. A party was armed and sailed for St Kilda, the intention being to take the sheep by force. But the St Kildans, armed with daggers and fishing-rods, attacked the invaders with such effect that the latter were forced to return to the mainland without attaining their object.

In sharp contrast, on another occasion the St Kildans experienced a few consecutive bad seasons and were unable to meet the rental demands. In 1780, MacLeod sent out a new boat to the islanders, assured them that their supply of seed corn and salt would be continued and allowed them some years' rent to enable the community to recover itself.

Communal Ownership

The internal organisation of the island community was based on socialistic principles. Its survival depended on a communal approach to all matters which affected the islanders as a recognisable corpus. Apart from the minister and his housekeeper, and the ground officer or deputy, who himself largely adhered to the communal code of living, no person on the island was allowed to assume authority over his neighbours. Even these persons exercised authority only very rarely when the occasion was serious enough to warrant an arbitrator and judge.

Primarily, the social regulator in St Kilda was the ensuring that the rents and dues owed to the owner were always paid. Each individual, and each family unit, were thus under a strict code of practice with little room for the exhibition of personal idiosyncrasies to satisfy any natural egocentric urge. All property on the island on which the livelihood of the islanders depended was held in common; this included boats, climbing ropes and fowling gear. As regards the boats, their maintenance was also on a communistic principle: each man was made responsible for the upkeep of a section of the boat.

Everything on St Kilda existed for the common good. Gifts brought in by tourists, philanthropists, visitors or the factor, were divided as equally as possible between the families. If this were not possible, lots were cast. The island's produce, and in particular the fulmar, which became the mainstay of the island's economy, was subjected to equal shares. The island's rocks used by the fulmars for breeding were divided into the number of families on the island, in much the same manner as was adopted by the North Rona community. During the breeding season, each man policed his lot to see that the birds were not molested; sheep in particular had to be kept from disturbing the birds. From August, the young birds were killed by the family, with assistance from the rest of the community as required. After each day's work, the fulmar harvest was placed in a heap, usually on the foreshore, and divided according to the number of households on the island. In keeping with the character of the St Kildan society, the sick and aged, who often lived alone, were not forgotten in the share-out. Until about 1880, the fulmar and the puffin were the only seabirds subject to this division, because they were, till that time, the two main sources of commodities for paying the rents.

All the grazing on the island was held in common. Each islander could keep as many sheep or cattle as he was personally able to pay rent for. Only on the island of Dun were there any restrictions on grazing facilities. The grass on Dun was used mainly for wintering lambs; because of its small acreage, it could accommodate only a small number of animals from each householder.

Social welfare appeared in the shape of insurance, in that should an islander lose a sheep, the loss was made good by the rest of the community in proportion to the amount held by each family. The participation in the bird-harvest of the sick, aged and infirm has already been mentioned.

Latterly, some fifty years before the evacuation of St Kilda, the principles which had for so long been the bases of the St Kildan method of government, began to deteriorate. Robert Connell, who visited the island in 1885–6, had this to say:

> In fishing, too, the St Kildans are socialists. As a rule, two boats of six men each go out to the fishing, and here again the produce is divided among the lucky sixteen (there were 16 crofts on the island). There are strong and willing men outside the charmed number, but they must stand aside in favour of the elect . . . it appears to be not far from the grossest selfishness, and tyranny and oppression of the weak. After fifteen days' stay on St Kilda I came to the deliberate conclusion that this nibbling at socialism is responsible for a good deal of the moral chaos which has so completely engulfed the islanders.

It has certainly done not a little to cripple the fishing industry. The four presentation boats which the islanders now possess are simply going to wreck in their hands, and one apparent reason is that they are common property. What is everybody's business is nobody's business, and so the boats are allowed to lie and rot uncared for on the beach. When next a begging letter comes for another boat the subscribing public should impose certain conditions with their gift. If a boat is ever given again it should be presented not to the community but to half-a-dozen of the most deserving members.

Island Laws

The islanders' body of customary law was largely based on the Mosaic code. In fact, so closely did it resemble its Mosaic counterpart that in 1758 MacAulay thought that missionaries had brought it to the island at an early date. Essentially a republic, the St Kildan community was governed by what came to be known as the 'St Kilda Parliament'. This body comprised all the adult males on the island and had power over all the actions of the whole community. No chairman was appointed 'and when differences of opinion arise as to the suitability of the work proposed for the day, the thread of debate is often lost in noise'.

The Parliament met each weekday morning to consider the work to be done for that day. No rules governed the conduct at these daily meetings. Each man arrived in his own time. Once convened the assembly would consider the type of work to be done : fishing, bird-catching, or visiting the neighbouring islands. John Ross, schoolmaster on St Kilda wrote in 1889 that the Parliament 'very much resembles our Honourable British Parliament in being able to waste any amount of precious time over a very small matter while on the other hand they can pass a Bill before it is well introduced'. But while the assembly wasted time on days when matters of little urgency required attention, it was quick to realise that time was important in the island's economy and could not be frittered away on talking. The weather, tides and seasons required prompt attention and quick action, and usually received it. Such an assembly, however, also generated gossip and many inter-family feuds resulted which, though their heat was temporarily dissipated during the communal work to be done, often survived for generations.

RELIGION AND INSTITUTIONS

Donald Monro, High Dean of the Isles, visited the islands of the Hebrides in 1549 and he mentioned St Kilda in his record. He tells of MacLeod of Harris, who sent his steward to the island every midsummer, with a chaplain to baptise the children. He further observes that the inhabitants were 'a simple and poor people and scarce learnt in any religion'. However, it can be taken that the basic elements of the Christian religion were introduced to the island at a very early date. But the passage of time altered the original form of belief. After his visit in 1838, Lachlan MacLean wrote:

> The religion of St Kilda for several centuries was, as we may suppose, a mixture of popery and druidism. Without teacher or taught, what could we expect? In the year 1641 a well-known leader of the clan MacDonald, Colla Ciotach, ie left-handed Coll, from having lost his right hand in battle, fled for his life to St Kilda. Here during a banishment of three-quarters of a year, he employed himself in teaching the natives the Lord's prayer, the Decalogue, and the Creed, in the popish style.
>
> In the year 1697, Mr Martin visited them, for three weeks. He was to them another Knox, in throwing down their altars and scourging their will-worship. The Highlander, inerudite as he may be, has, however, about him some good points not unworthy the imitation of the citizen: even in Martin's time they assembled in the church-yard on the Lord's day in the morning, there they said the Lord's prayer, Creed, and Ten Commandments. They dropped work on Saturday at 12 o'clock noon, and would work at nothing till Monday. When a death took place in the island, all work was at a stand till after the interment. They believed in God the Father, the Son, and Holy Ghost, as also in Flathinnis, the island of the brave, and Ii bhroin, the region of sorrow. They rose in the morning and commenced their labour by invoking the name of God, and swearing was not known amongst them.

During the autumn of 1705 the General Assembly of the Church of Scotland, commiserating the deplorable state of St Kilda, sent Mr Alexander Buchan to the island as a catechist. Buchan lived among the islanders for four years spending his time bringing his flock to an acceptable level of belief. His success caught the attention of the new-formed Society in Scotland for propagating Christian Knowledge (SSPCK), which was just beginning its eventful career in the Highlands. The Society ordained Mr Buchan and sent him back to St Kilda to continue the spiritual nourishment of its islanders. This he did until his death in 1730. During his ministry, on a stipend of 300 merks (£16 13 4d—£16·66), he constructed the first manse, started the first library and raised the islanders to the level of thinking beings. His wife was responsible for teaching the island women how to knit.

In 1758 the Rev Kenneth MacAulay was sent as missionary; he published a history of St Kilda in 1764. A succession of ministers followed including the Rev John MacDonald who first visited St Kilda in 1822. He found neither an organised Church nor strong Calvinist religion. The manse had fallen into a ruinous state and the people assembled in a barn for their services. MacDonald laid the foundations of a highly organised, strictly puritanical and harsh religion. For his similar work in the Highlands he was given the title of 'Apostle of the North'. He said on his first visit to St Kilda:

> Swearing is too prevalent among them and its common expressions, such as by the soul, by Mary, by the book . . . and what is worse, by the sacred name seem to be quite familiar with them on every occasion . . . It grieves me to say and I took pains to ascertain the truth that among the whole body I did not find a single individual who could be truly called a decidedly religious person; that is one who has felt the influence of the truth on his soul, and who exhibits that influence in his life and conversation.

To put matters right he paid another visit in 1824, and two further visits before he finally left the island in the care of the Rev Neil MacKenzie in 1830. The Rev MacKenzie's fourteen-year tenure of office as resident minister was noted for his attention, not only to the spiritual needs of the islanders, but also to their moral and physical wants. If the spiritual level had been raised by MacDonald, MacKenzie raised the standard of living. It was through his efforts that the island's housing was improved. He went to Glasgow and returned with beds, chairs, stools, and glass windows.

The old church was in such a state of ruin that a new building had to be erected with a neat one-storey slated manse at the end of it. The cost of the work was £600.

When MacKenzie left St Kilda in 1844, to take up a new charge in Argyll, his departure marked the end of what might be called an era of franchise in religious belief. The Disruption, which took place in Edinburgh in 1843, took a year to reach St Kilda. The islanders were quickly won over to the dogmas of the Free Church and remained faithful to them until the evacuation in 1930. For the decade 1853–63, the St Kildans were under the charge of a catechist, Duncan Kennedy. He was succeeded by the Rev Cameron who, after two years' stay, handed over the ministry to the Rev John MacKay. MacKay was at one time a schoolmaster and was ordained to the ministry only with the view to his being sent to St Kilda.

MacKay's term of office lasted for twenty-four years, until a dispute occurred among the islanders; he was pensioned off and his place taken by a younger licenciate, Angus Fiddes. In MacKay's charge, the islanders allowed their religious beliefs to rule their entire way of life. In a less harsh environment, the community might have survived better than it did; other communities with a more professed adherence to religious belief have survived until the present day. But St Kilda a century ago was not the place nor the time for lives to be governed by strict religious dogma. MacKay pressed the islanders hard, so much so that the result came under the attack of two of St Kilda's most famous writers, John Sands and Robert Connell. Both men concentrated on the debilitating effects of MacKay's over-strict rule of the islanders and his position as uncrowned king, with his unmarried housekeeper as a 'dominating queen'. When, in 1877, George Seton took a supply of innocuous children's books to the island, MacKay immediately imposed his censorship on them and the island children went without their books. Wrote Sands of MacKay:

> The weak-minded pope and prime minister rolled into one who rules the destinies of the island has reduced religion into a mere hypocritical formalism, finding no place in his creed for self-reliance or any of the manlier virtues . . . It is nothing to Mr MacKay whether the poor people starve their crofts or neglect the fishing so long as his own silly fads are observed.

The islanders, however, seemed happy with their spiritual lot, though they realised that the demands made on them to tread the narrow path defined by MacKay would eventually bring their island economy to a critical state with complete evacuation as the only alternative. It has been said that life on St Kilda was in itself a religion of sorts. Certainly, towards the end of the island's history of human inhabitation, amid a world full of material benefits, it required a strong faith to remain on St Kilda. This faith was inherent in the St Kildan make-up, the legacy of many generations, and fitted in extremely well both with the ministers who were sent to the island and with the dogmas which the islanders were taught to accept. The St Kildans were sincere in their beliefs and were equally true to them in their actions. Such a faith still exists in many areas of the Scottish Highlands and Islands.

When Angus Fiddes took over from MacKay in 1889, there began a new régime of change in the island. Fiddes was a broad-minded man. With persistence and patience he succeeded in rooting out the scourge of the 'eight-days' sickness' which had plagued the island for a century. He also tried to get the St Kildans to plant trees. But the islanders refused on the grounds that the trees would take up good ground where sheep might otherwise graze. The stringency of religion was not lessened under Fiddes; some of his sermons lasted for four hours.

The Rev Fiddes was the last ordained Free Church minister to serve St Kilda. After he had filled his term of office in 1903, a succession of missionaries followed who, reflecting the enlightenment of the twentieth century, eased the terror of religion and attended more to the medical and material wants of their charges.

Marriage

The form of marriage used in St Kilda in 1697 is described by Martin Martin. The couple who wished to be married were taken to the marriage-stool and, in front of the assembled islanders, asked whether there were any objections to their marriage. If there were none, the couple were asked if they were willing to live together in weal or woe. After the assent, the official performing the marriage, who was usually the steward's resident officer, took out his naked dirk and caused the couple to swear on it. They were then declared married. Fifteen couples were married in this way on 17 June 1697.

The Rev Neil MacKenzie, minister during the 1830s, describes a marriage at which he officiated:

> In the evening we were invited to the village to a Reiteach (agreement) between the young folk, with which we complied. On our arrival we found all the men of the island sitting on the ground, or rather reclining close to the walls of the house of the bride's father, on each side feet to feet, so that it was very difficult to get through them. The near female relatives were in the upper appartment with the bride. We were seated on a chest among the men. A glass of spirits was handed round by the bride's father, commencing with us and going round the whole. A short and desultory conversation ensued, and then we separated. Not a person mentioned the reason of our coming together, except drinking to the health of the young folk.
>
> On Sabbath-day they were proclaimed three several times, for they were not inclined to wait for three Sabbath-days; they were therefore exposed to pay three shillings instead of one, which is thus divided—one shilling to the precentor, sixpence to the person who proclaims them, and the rest to the poor. Early on Monday morning two young men were despatched to the hill to catch sheep; a certain quantity of barley grain was given to the girls to be ground and baked; two elderly men were appointed to boil the beef, and the rest skulked about the houses, or lent a hand as need required . . . A considerable number of the villagers attended the marriage sermon. As soon as they were married they (the couple) went home; and we saw no more of them till after tea, when the governor of the feast, the bride's brother, came, dressed, in the uniform, (which is a rag of white cotton cloth sewed to each shoulder

> and the front of his bonnet) to invite us to the marriage feast . . . When we went we found every man in the island seated in the house of the bride's father, with a table of planks before them; the ground served them for seats. One end of the board was raised much higher; this was intended for us, with a chest for a seat, and opposite to us were the bride and bridegroom and their friends. On the board before us were placed three plates, (a very unusual thing in St Kilda) one filled with mutton, one filled with barley bannocks, and the third filled with cheese. The rest had their mutton and bread in wooden dishes made by nailing small boards together. There was neither soup nor drink of any kind on the board, nor used at any of their feasts. After a blessing was pronounced, no conversation for a while interrupted their eating, but afterwards there was some general conversation. When we came out, the women and boys were lounging about the house; the former waiting to get a piece of bread and mutton as a reward for their baking and grinding. Their portion being given out to them, the boys were seated at the table to consume what remained; when these were removed, all went home.

The Rev MacKenzie also had a case of breach of promise to deal with. It was tried in open court at the end of the church, before the ministers and elders. The lady proved her case against the truant and he was fined, not a cash sum, but a hundred full-grown fulmars, fifty young solan geese and a hair rope as a solatium, and a tocher (dowry) in the next matrimonial venture. The hair rope was by far the most important part of the fine; it was a prized possession necessary for bird-catching.

Death

Death on St Kilda was a solemn occasion, with those overtones which are characteristic only of small communities. Again, the Rev MacKenzie supplies the picture of a burial during the 1830s:

> When it is known that death has really taken place, the near relatives and others cry, and weep and wail. Who on such an occasion could refrain from tears? Yet even grief and mourning should have their bounds; but here for a time they seem to have none; to calm them is impracticable. In a short time,

however, they separate, and some of those who seemed comfortless are nearly as cheerful as ever. This is the case with the females, for the men in general have more regard to propriety.

They do not in general keep their dead above two or three days in the house; during that time two or three persons who can handle wood better than the rest are busily engaged in making a coffin. Two more go to the hill for sheep belonging to the deceased, or if he had none, one of his near relatives supplies sheep to be used at the funeral, and the rest of the inhabitants stand looking on, or sauntering about the houses, for they will do no work when a dead body is in the village. The women, at the same time, are as busily grinding and baking as if preparing a marriage feast. These preparations are for food to those that watch the corpse (which they assiduously do till interred), for a feast of bread and mutton or beef, which they take in the burying-ground, and a portion for the women who prepared the meat. The more sheep and cows they kill, and the more barley they use, the more honour do they intend to confer on their deceased friend. Those who have lost many relatives have been much reduced by this foolish custom.

When all things are in readiness for the internment, a few of the young men set off to a distance to get a broad turf for a covering to the grave, while the rest are digging it. They then come to the house and get the coffin well tied on two sticks, and carry it in the course of the sun round the gardens with which the group of houses which form the village are surrounded, though they should go through their corn. As soon as the grave is filled up, they sit down, summer or winter, upon the grass or stones, and eat the bread and beef which had been prepared; and if any of them be detained at home, their portion is sent. If the deceased be an adult, he is interred in the afternoon; and if a child, late in the evening.

Pastimes

In common with all remote communities, the islanders relied on their own talents for their entertainment and amusement. Before the advent of the Free Church to the island, the St Kildans were 'very fond of music, dancing to an old wretched fiddle with great delight. They were also good singers, and accompanied all their duties with suitable songs, generally of their own composition.' Martin Martin says that the islanders played the Jews harp which 'disposed them to dance mightily'; and when they brewed produced an ale which likewise 'when drunk plentifully disposes them to dance merrily'. The islanders were also given much to games, particularly shinty. Rock-climbing was as much a sport as an economic activity.

FOLKLORE

Folklore is the survival of the thought and ways of life of former times. It is basically knowledge mostly preserved by oral communication and generally divorced effectively from the more rationally-based knowledge of less superstitious people. Superstition (Latin: *super* = above; *stare* = to stand) means a standing-over or a survival of an irrational or credulous attitude towards magico-religious beliefs and practices of a civilised community, long after these primitive ideas and customs have been abandoned by the more sophisticated sections of society.

On approaching the subject of folklore and superstitious beliefs in a small, well-insulated community such as St Kilda, one looks for indications of an accretion of knowledge and beliefs over many centuries which could be related to the development of the community from its primitive beginnings to a more sophisticated outlook on life and living.

In the main, however, one is disappointed with the survivals of folklore and superstitious belief in St Kilda. One might have expected interesting and significant idiosyncrasies, laterals of general Scottish Highland folklore showing St Kildan characteristics. Instead, the ground is sparsely populated and virtually echoes the general body of lore found on the Gaelic mainland of Scotland and in Eire. One reason may well be the continuing crass ignorance of the St Kildans in failing to recognise the value of strengthening oral methods of folklore preservation with the occasional literary record. Again, the community may have been too small; but this should not be accepted as the sole reason as even a single family can accrete a kind of folklore throughout succeeding generations. The influence of immigrants to St Kilda over the centuries might also account for the St Kildan body of lore and belief lacking some really individual characteristics. In summary, while the islanders were for centuries hedged in with superstition and customs which prevented progress to more rational planes of thinking, they failed to produce the stuff by which their island can be assessed in individualistic social terms.

Norse Legend

While many communities in Eire and Gaelic Scotland have origins deep in prehistory, or in Celtic mythology with claims to some connections with Celtic heroes, St Kilda can go back little more than one millenium, to the days when the Norse influence was being felt on the western seaboard of Scotland. The King of Lochlainn (Norway) features prominently in all Gaelic folktales; St Kilda lays claim to an association with a son of his. This son was wrecked on a rock to the west of Hirt. He came ashore in a small boat and made for a water-brook close by the site of the present church. Here the St Kildans found him and, while he drank deeply to wash the sea's salt out of his mouth and lungs, they caught him by the neck and held his head under the water until he drowned. The rock on which he was wrecked was called Sgeir Mac Righ Lochlainn (rock of the son of the King of Norway) and was named thus until at least the turn of this century. The son of the king always came off second best in other parts of Scotland; in St Kilda he fared no better.

Fairies

The ubiquitous fairies found their way to St Kilda. Their presence on the island group is confirmed by a number of stories, though the St Kildan fairy seems no different from his counterpart on the Scottish mainland.

The subterranean dwellings in Gleann Mor were regarded as the habitat of the St Kildan fairies. Calum Mor's house was built by Calum, or Big Malcolm, who was lame and, with the aid of supernatural help, finished the construction all in one day. In another time two islanders passed a green knoll, from the centre of which they heard a noise. They paused and while they listened a door opened and a fairy woman emerged to offer each of them a bowl of milk. One man accepted her generosity, crossing him-

Page 53: *(left)* Stac Lee, St Kilda; *(right)* Landing stores on the east cliffs of Toa Rona, North Rona

Page 54 North Rona: *(above)* remains of a dwelling-house; *(below)* the entrance to the church. Quern-stones are lying on the left

self while he did so in the name of the Father, Son and Holy Ghost. The act was an insult to the fairy who withdrew her offer and disappeared into the knoll.

One woman working in the harvest field by the light of a St Kildan moon, left her child on a fairy mound. When she returned to the mound her child had been replaced by a fairy changeling. Another mother was visited by two fairy women clad in green. Seeing the child in her arms, they enchanted her and robbed her of power of speech, but she heard the fairies discuss together the gift of fluency of tongue which they were about to bestow on the child. In later years this child grew to become one of the most fluent persons on the island, with the ability to out-talk a dozen people without feeling any fatigue.

The Water-bull

The *tarbh uisge* (water-bull) was another supernatural creature found in St Kilda as on the Scottish mainland and Western Isles. One day a St Kildan woman was gathering peats when a door opened in a small hillock. Full of curiosity, but at the same time being extremely cautious, she stuck a small iron knife into the ground beside the door and peered into the interior of the mound. To her amazement she saw a tiny speckled cow give birth to a speckled calf without ears—the sure sign of the malevolent water-bull spirit.

Stones

Belief in the supernatural is associated with the Clach an Eolas, the stone of knowledge. Supposedly, if any man stood on the stone on the first day of the quarter he would receive second sight and would be able to see all that was to happen in the ensuing quarter. Another stone which featured prominently in the island's tradition was the *clach dotaig*, a semi-transparent stone which, both in St Kilda and in many other parts of the Highlands and Islands, was held in reverence. To obtain this 'stone of virtues', one had to boil a raven's egg and once boiled return it to the parent nest. In time the parent bird would become so impatient for the egg to hatch that it would fly off to return with this stone which a diligent observer could secure as his treasured possession.

Yet another stone on St Kilda with superstitious association was that mentioned by MacAulay (1758). This stone was large, square and white in colour; it was located on the face of a small rise between the village and the north-west side of Hirt. The St Kildans used to pour libations of milk into an indentation in this stone each Sunday. The deity associated with the stone was the *gruagach*, a supernatural being who, on the Scottish mainland, was supposed to have once been a woman of good family put under a spell and given a kind of fairy nature. It was the duty of these beings (there were many of them) to be interested in cattle and the dairy, and in the affairs of the house to which they were attached. The libations of milk ensured the fertility of the island's cattle and that no harm would come to them or to the products from their milk yield. MacAulay also mentions that some little way above this stone was a small plain green, *tigh an triar*, where the islanders prayed for blessings upon their cattle and where they used to sanctify them with salt, water and fire, when removing them from one grazing to another.

Below this plain was another with much the same character which the islanders would never convert into arable ground believing it to be the abode of some forgotten deity; any attempt to disturb it would at once be punished by the loss of the island boat or some other calamity. MacAulay says:

> Here the old St Kildans implored the blessing of God on their cattle, and here they lustrated or sanctified these cattle with salt, water and fire. By virtue of this ceremony they conjured away, or so they fondly thought, the power of fascinations, the malignity of elves, and the vengeance of every evil genius.

Various accounts written of St Kilda mention that sacrifices were once offered to the God of the Seasons on a rising on Hirt called Mullach-geal.

A stone more associated with custom and tradition rather than superstition was the Lover's Stone. This is at the south-west corner of the island, overlooking Soay. It is a lofty pinnacle, a high perpendicular precipice some 200 ft above the sea. This had to be climbed by all aspirants to St Kildan girls in marriage. On reaching the top, the lover had to plant his left heel on the outer edge, with the sole of his foot entirely unsupported, and then to extend his right leg forward. The right foot had to be grasped with both hands for a time deemed long enough to prove his courage and ability to climb the other crags of St Kilda for the harvest of birds.

Wells

The wells on St Kilda had their inevitable associations with the supernatural, a possible carry-over from the beliefs in animism which were widespread among the peoples of Britain before the advent of Christianity. Tobar na Buadh (well of virtue) is located at the foot of the great glen and some thirty yards from where Amhuinn a' Ghlinne (river of the glen) enters the sea. 'It was a fundamental article of faith,' says MacAulay, 'the water here was a sovereign cure for a great variety of distempers, deafness particularly, and every disease.' At one time there was an altar close by the well where a prayer was offered to the deity; no one approached this well with empty hands. This well was far-famed. Martin Martin first recorded it as being the 'finest of the excellent fountains or springs in which St Kilda abounds'. The more active tourists of three centuries later landing on the island from the *Hebrides* or the *Dunara Castle* used to dash for the col between Mullach Sgar and Mullach-geal to drink the well waters.

Another popular well was Tobar na Cille, sometimes called the well of St Brendan. This well was resorted to when the wind was in the wrong direction and prevented the islanders from launching their boat. The direction of the wind altered in the islanders' favour when each man about to put to sea stood astride the well waters for a few seconds.

Feast Days

The St Kildan calendar of holidays included six main feasts: St Columba, St Brendan, Christmas, New Year's Day, Easter and Michaelmas. Significantly, St Kilda himself is not remembered. On the saints' days, all the milk in the island was given to the factor's deputy who thereupon divided it equally and impartially between every man, woman and child. On Christmas and New Year's Day the St Kildans ate the best food they could afford and drank liberally and 'danced with vigour'. Easter was observed in a solemn and quiet manner while Michaelmas was a kind of Derby Day, similar to the horse races which once took place in North Uist. Again this custom looks much like an importation from that island. On this particular feast day, a procession was formed on the shore. All those who had horses were mounted, without saddle or bridle, and had only a wisp of straw to guide the horse's head. The procession went as far as the houses, when the horses returned to the shore for those who had been left behind; this went on until everyone in the island had taken part in the proceedings. It was also the custom on St Michael's Day to prepare in each family a large loaf of bread, dedicated to the saint, and divided among the members of the family.

Second Sight

The instances of second sight in St Kilda are mainly concerned with the foretelling of death and the description of the funeral or progress of a coffin. These instances parallel with those recorded for other parts of the Hebrides, particularly the Southern Isles.

Duigan and Fearchar Mor

The story of these two men is one of the few tales of truly St Kildan origin. The Rev Neil MacKenzie (minister of St Kilda *c* 1830) tells the tale:

> . . . Several hundred years ago, two men from Lewis, Duigan and Fearchar Mor visited St Kilda. On a certain day the two went up to the top of Aois-mheall: they were no sooner up than down they came in a flurry, crying that the Sassenachs were coming, and, in the same breath, imploring the poor simple natives, who believed them implicitly, to betake themselves to the chapel—to the horns of the altar, the sanctity of which, they said, would save them. The inhabitants were no sooner in the chapel than the Lewis-men secured the door—set fire to the fabric, and burned everyone living in the island except one old woman who happened to be absent. This woman, smelling

> that all was not right, concealed herself in a cave on the south side of the bay, preserving life for several months by stealing during the night from the ruffian's store. The Land Steward's birlinn was seen at the set time making towards the island; the two men hurried to the beach to meet him and tell him a made-up tale; by this time the solitary woman had made her appearance—the men were astonished—the secret was disclosed—the steward gave his verdict, namely, that Duigan and Fearchar Mor be both left upon Stac an Armin where they could get nothing but raw birds. Upon reaching Stac an Armin, Fearchar Mor said to Duigan, 'Do not forget your flint and steel.' On hearing this the steward seized the fire-raisers, which when Fearchar Mor saw he gave a desperate leap into the fathomless main and was seen no more! Duigan was left on Soay, where he built a wall, to protect him from the north wind, which bears his name to this day, as also the cave in which he spent the remainder of his sorry existence.

In this tradition, it is said that the old woman was taken off St Kilda and for some time, until repopulated with fresh stock, the island was deserted.

Perhaps the one solitary instance of an exclusive St Kildan legend is that of the 'Amazon'. Her house is known today as the *Tigh na Banaghaisgich* or female warrior's house (see page 101). It has been known in Gleann Mor since Martin Martin gave us the first authentic description of St Kilda in 1697. The Amazon's house was a focal point in St Kildan tradition. Martin mentions that there were many traditions connected with this lady but—'I shall trouble my Reader with no more of them'.

POETRY AND SONG

When Robert Connell, of the *Glasgow Herald*, made his visits to St Kilda in 1885 and 1886, he endeavoured without much success to collect what original poetical fragments remained in oral circulation among the islanders. Martin writes of 'some of both sexes who have a genius for poetry, and are great admirers of music'. Most other writers have, however, indicated that the St Kildans were given credit for possessing a higher degree of intellect than was in fact the case. Even so, there do exist a number of fragments of song and poetry which prove that the islanders had inherited enough of the gift of the Celt in the world of word and music to produce the occasional gem showing interesting or original poetic imagery. Out of hand, Dr Johnson, while on his tour of the Hebrides (he was once offered the chance to buy the island of St Kilda but refused), declared that no good poetry could come from St Kilda, perhaps thinking that a community must needs be considerably larger in order to generate, contain and nourish the creative elements which are necessary to produce the cultural background of any community.

As might be expected, the St Kildan songs and poetry find their roots in the daily life and experiences of the islanders. One set of verses (all poetry and songs were in Gaelic) was composed by a St Kildan woman whose husband and son set out for the strait between Hirt and Dun to catch guillemots. Despite precautions taken by the father for his son's safety, the latter fell over a precipice into the sea and was drowned. Robert Connell remarks that the verses of poetry he found were nearly all pitched in a minor key.

The collection of Gaelic hymns, incantations and fragments of verse by Alexander Carmichael, *Carmina Gadelica*, contains some examples of St Kildan poetry. Carmichael, who spent many years in the Hebrides recording and collecting much of what would now be lost had it not been for his intense interest in the subject, writes of one reciter whom he met in 1865 :

> The technique and diction of the following pieces would not satisfy Johnson, but they have other qualities that might please him. Though not old, they have a charming simplicity and intense feeling. There are some . . . which the writer took down on 22nd May 1865 from the recitation of Eibhrig Nic Cruimein, Euphemia MacCrimmon, cottar, aged eighty-four years, who had many old songs, stories and traditions of the island . . . The aged reciter was much censured for her recital of these songs and poems, and the writer for causing the old woman to stir the recesses of her memory for this lore; for the people of St Kilda have now discarded songs and music, dancing, folklore, and the stories of the foolish past.

The following 'St Kilda Lilt', in the form of a dialogue, was composed by Euphemia MacCrimmon's father and mother before they were married:

HE:

Away bent spade, away straight spade,
  Away each goat and sheep and lamb;
Up my rope, up my snare—
  I have heard the gannet upon the sea!
Thanks to the Being, the gannets are come,
Yes, and the big birds along with them;
  Dark dusky maid, a cow in the fold!
A brown cow, a brown cow, a brown cow beloved,
A brown cow, my dear one, that would milk the milk for
  thee,
Ho ro ru ra ree, playful maid,
  Dark dusky maid, cow in the fold!
  The birds are a-coming, I hear their tune!

SHE:

Truly my sweetheart is the herdsman
Who would threaten the staff and would not strike!

HE:

Mary, my dear love is the maid,
Though dark her locks her body is fragrant!

SHE:

Thou art my handsome joy, thou art my sweetheart,
Thou gavest me first the honied fulmar!

HE:

Thou art my turtle-dove, thou art my mavis,
Thou are my melodious harp in the sweet morning.

SHE:

Thou art my hero, thou art my basking sunfish,
Thou gavest me the puffin and the black-headed guillemot.

HE:

The mirth of my eyes and the essence of my joy thou art,
And my sweet-sounding lyre in the mountain of mist.

The following song or lament 'It was no crew of landsmen', was composed to commemmorate the death of eighteen St Kildans on their return from a mercy food mission to North Uist:

It was no crew of landsmen
Crossed the ferry on Wednesday:
'Tis tidings of disaster if you live not.

What has kept you so long from me?
Is the high sea and the sudden wind catching you,
So that you could not at once give her sail.

'Tis a profitless journey
That took the noble man away,
To take our one son from me and from Donald.

My son and my three brothers are gone,
And the one son of my mother's sister,
And, sorest tale, that will come or has come, my husband.

What has set me to draw ashes
And to take a spell at digging
Is that the men are away with no word of their living.

I am left without fun or merriment
Sitting on the floor of the glen;
My eyes are wet, oft are tears on them.

Closer to the workaday life of the islanders are the working or labour songs, of which the following St Kilda waulking song, is typical:

I would make the fair cloth for thee,
Thread as the thatch-rope stout.

I would make the feathered buskin for thee,
Thou beloved and importunate of men.

I would give thee the precious anchor,
And the family gear which my grandfather had.

My love is the hunter of the bird,
Who earliest comes over misty sea.

My love the sailor of the waves,
Great the cheer his brow will show.

EDUCATION

The St Kildan community, always functional in its approach to life, held education in no great esteem. When, during the reign of Queen Anne, the Rev Alexander Buchan was sent to the island he did manage to educate some of the boys. Fifty years later, in 1758, the Rev MacAulay found all but four of the islanders illiterate. But by the 1880s, there was scarcely a child of six years old on the island who could not read at least one portion of the Bible.

Education, as a formal function of society, first came to St Kilda in 1709, when a Charity School was set up. It was financed and managed by the Society in Scotland for Propagating Christian Knowledge (SSPCK). The school had a chequered history. In a return for 1714, concerning the number of children attending the society's schools, there was 'no account this year for Hirta'. In 1727: 'At Hirta, alias St Kilda, an island and parish in the Presbytery of Longisland . . . the greatest number of scholars at once there is only 28.' A century later the school on the island fell under the management of the Gaelic School Society. There were 44 scholars: 26 males and 18 females. 6 of the males, of whom 3 were married, were aged between 20 and 40 years. Of the females, 6 were between the ages of 20 and 30. When the 1861 Census was taken, only 2 islanders, neither St Kildan by birth, could speak English; and only 2 were able to sign their names. Thus it is plain that, until 1884, education on St Kilda was a sporadic matter and was entirely dependent on the attitude and interest shown by the resident missionary.

In the summer of 1884, the first schoolmaster arrived on St Kilda. The presence of Mr Campbell was the result of an application made to the secretary of the Ladies Association of the Highland Society. Campbell's school was a room in the factor's house. There was a quick succession of teachers (six in all) between 1884 and 1888. In 1888, there were 14 schoolchildren on the island: 10 boys and 4 girls, all at various stages of learning. Besides grammar, the subjects taught were geography, history, arithmetic, and composition. One boy was sufficiently well advanced to be able to learn some Latin. The pupils were divided into three groups or 'classes': Senior, Intermediate, and Junior. In 1892, there were 19 schoolchildren most of whom were under the age of 14 years. By 1898, when Norman Heathcote visited St Kilda for a study of the island's natural history, the children could speak English well. The year before had seen the foundations of the island's new schoolhouse laid with full Masonic honours. By 1899 the building was completed. In 1906, when the number of children attending school had risen to twenty-two, St Kilda saw the dawn of a new era in education with the advent of Mr and Mrs MacLauchlan.

Under the supervision of this man-and-wife team, education took on many practical aspects. School began at 10 o'clock and finished at 4 o'clock, with an hour's break for lunch. Mr MacLauchlan took the morning classes while his wife took those in the afternoon. They found the islanders, particularly the young ones, eager to learn. The young girls, with their mothers, were taught to make clothing in an island where the tailoring had previously been done by the men. The increase in the islanders' facility with the English language proved of value when the tourist trade brought visitors to the island. No efforts were made, however, to teach the islanders how to improve their cloth-making (tweed) techniques, their husbandry, or their crops by the use of artificial fertilisers.

An interesting document, the *St Kilda School Log Book* is preserved by Highland Regional Council library archives, which authority took over from Inverness-shire County Council, once responsible for the education provisions on the island. It reveals life on the island from the days of the first school to the last entries in 1930:

1906, Oct 3—No school for three days owing to the sad death by drowning of Norman Gillies, one of the VI Str pupils. Great gloom over the island.
1909, Mar 22—Great drowning accident; school closed for seven days.
1916, Aug 22—A sad accident occurred while after the fulmar and two men lost their lives. Owing to this the school was not open yesterday.
1918, 10 Dec—School reopened today. No school has been held

since the island was bombarded (by a German submarine) on 15th May. During most of that time the school has been occupied by a party from the naval station while their own premises have been repaired.

1930, 12 June—No school today. Mr Tom Johnston, M.P., Under Secretary for Scotland with other representatives of the Government visited the island in connection with the evacuation. A general meeting was held in the school.

1930, June—Attendance perfect for last week. (Eight). School closed today with a small treat which the children seemed thoroughly to enjoy. Today probably ends the school in St Kilda as all the inhabitants intend leaving the island this summer. I hope to be away soon.

Thus ends the logbook, to the tune of an old song: the desertion of an island. The school itself was classed as the 'St Kilda Sub-School, conducted under Art. 19 of the Scotch Code and is under Obbe Public School, Harris, for the purpose of that Article.'

MEDICAL SERVICES

The medical history of St Kilda is full of paradoxes. For instance, while other small isolated communities tended to suffer from intermarriage and inbreeding, the St Kildans were remarkable in showing no ill-effects from consanguineous marriages. In the *Edinburgh Medical Journal* of April 1865, it was noted that of the fourteen married couples on St Kilda at that time, in not one case was the relationship that of full cousins. In five couples the relationship was that of second cousin, and to these fifty-four children had been born. Thirty-seven of these had died in infancy as the result of disease; of the remaining seventeen, not one was in any way abnormal, either physically or mentally. In 1878, Sands remarked: 'Although they have intermarried possibly for a thousand years, none of the pernicious effects that one has been taught to expect has resulted.' The fact is that the St Kildans themselves were fully aware of the effects of inbreeding and, like many primitive societies, exercised strict control on marriages. In addition, the resident minister or missionary saw to it that couples who wanted to marry were not too closely related. A further reason for the virtual absence of the effects of intermarriage between close cousins was the occasional sally to the main Hebridean islands by St Kildans in search of wives.

In 1697 Martin Martin observed that the children of the island were so strong and agile that, even at the age of three, they were able to scale the walls of the old 'black houses' with little difficulty. By the twentieth century, however, the St Kildans suffered from debilitating weakness, evidenced by the increased incidence of rheumatism, colds and headaches. Medical observers saw a physical deterioration, no doubt brought about by the increased frequency of contacts with tourists and visitors who must have brought to the island illnesses which the St Kildans were not able to fight off, lacking the necessary immunity.

Disease, in one form or another, looms large in the island's medical history. In 1684 leprosy struck hard and was still in evidence when Martin visited St Kilda thirteen years later. In 1724 a smallpox epidemic virtually wiped out the community. According to one source of information, an old St Kilda man, Donald MacDonald, went to Harris where he died of smallpox. The following year his clothes were brought back to St Kilda by a relation and immediately the whole community went down with the disease. Only four adults and twenty-six orphaned children managed to survive the epidemic, the only survivors out of twenty-five families.

It was a miraculous survival, of which the Rev Neil MacKenzie wrote:

> The disease . . . which caused by far the greatest mortality was a visitation of smallpox. It was brought to the island in the clothes of one of their number who died of the disease in Harris. It broke out just after a party had been left on Stack-an-Armin to collect feathers. At such times they generally remain away for about ten days. Before that time expired the disease had made such progress that there were not in health a sufficient number to form a crew. Death after death followed. At last there was scarcely sufficient left to bury the dead. As they had then no spades, one man is said to have dug eleven graves with the back board of a wool card about 18 inches by 9 in size. No coffins were attempted. So weak were the survivors, that when the dead bodies sometimes fell off the planks on

> which they were being carried, they were unable to raise them up again, and had to drag them to their graves. The hand of death was heavy on the place; out of twenty-five families only five could keep a fire. There were ninety-four deaths. When the factor came next summer he found those who had been left on Stack-an-Armin all well. They lived on fish and fowls, but at times suffered much from cold and hunger. They made fish-hooks out of a few rusty nails, and also contrived to stitch together their clothing with feathers and patch them with the skins of birds. They returned mostly to empty houses, crops generally never reaped, and the cattle roaming about half wild.

In 1832 there was an epidemic of cholera, though the population remained stable through the period of the disease. In 1913 another epidemic, of influenza and pneumonia, paralysed island life. Notice of the illnesses was sent to the Local Government Board in Edinburgh and arrangements were made with the Admiralty to dispatch a cruiser, HMS *Active*, with medical aid and food to the island. Two of the officers of the Board and two nurses joined the vessel at Oban. By the time the party had reached St Kilda most of the islanders were convalescing from influenza of the bronchial type. Most of the women and children had been acutely ill and highly fevered. In several houses, the entire family was prostrated, with as many as eight people, including children, in bed in the same room. Windows were tightly sealed. As no one had been available to cook food or even to milk the cows for several days, the condition of the people was pitiable. The church was cleaned, disinfected and converted into a temporary hospital and the adjoining school room was used as store room and kitchen. All the islanders recovered. The source of the epidemic was never discovered.

In general, the islanders were physically fit and suffered no more nor less than those in larger mainland communities. In 1830 the people were described as 'slender of form with fair hair and a florid complexion. On the whole they are good-looking. The diseases to which they are most subject are spotted fever, dyspepsia, and nervous disorders, with swelling and bowing of their limbs.'

In 1877 the islanders were '. . . of moderate stature; the men between 65 inches and 67½ inches tall, looked healthy and well fed, though rather flabby. The prevalent disease was rheumatism and dyspepsia was also common.' Towards 1890 the children on the island '. . . were anaemic and languid, suffering from symptoms of incipient scurvy'.

One illness which was not native to the island was the 'boat cold'. The St Kildans' affinity for this illness was an example of their lack of immunity to imported germs. The 'boat cold' was not quite confined to St Kilda: other remote islands such as Foula and Fair Isle experienced this peculiar instance of a community contracting disease from visitors. The illness was seldom fatal, though the occasional death did occur. The more important effect of the illness was the manner in which it could interrupt the routine of the island. Work was often made impossible, sometimes for weeks.

By far the most ravaging of diseases was that which struck at newborn infants and killed them before they had lived eight days. This was the 'sickness of eight days', or tetanus infantus. The first mention of the disease was made by MacAulay in 1756, though the disease was known and experienced before this date. Accurate records were not kept until the era of the Rev Neil MacKenzie, resident minister from July 1830 to October 1844. During this period of 14 years there were 68 deaths on the island. Of these, 37 were infant deaths (26 male: 11 female) thirty-two of them being the result of tetanus. What was even more saddening to the community was that of the 32 babes who died of tetanus, 23 were male children. According to the *British & Foreign Medico-Chirurgical Review* of 1838, eight out of every ten babies born on St Kilda died of tetanus.

With the island's ecclesiastics declaring that the disease was the way in which God controlled the population of the island and punished the wicked, the disease was accepted. When Miss Emily MacLeod visited the island in 1877 she was told, after suggesting that a trained nurse be sent to St Kilda: 'If it is God's will that babies should die nothing you can do will save them.' It was, strangely, left to the Rev Angus Fiddes to reverse the preaching of his predecessors and show that the cause of the disease was Man not God. In 1890 he applied to Glasgow for help in the form of a trained nurse. A nurse did arrive and stayed ten months, but she did not achieve much. The reason for her failure was that she had to remove centuries of tradition, in particular the rites carried out on the severed umbilical cord by a *bean-ghluine* or 'knee-woman' who was always present at the moment of birth and acted as midwife. This rite took the form of covering the severed umbilicus with a mixture of fulmar oil and dung. On many other islands with the same ritual, butter was used, but this was a scarce commodity in St Kilda and the islanders used their own deadly concoction. Suspecting that this was the source of the disease, Fiddes took a course in midwifery.

In the *Glasgow Medical Journal* of 1894, Dr Turner of Glasgow, who tutored Fiddes in midwifery, wrote:

> Considering that what theoretically would be likely to give the best chance to escape the disease would be the careful antiseptic treatment of the cord, I gave Mr Fiddes instructions for the application of iodoform freely to it, when it was first dressed, for it to be rolled up in iodoform gauze, the whole to be covered with a large pad of sublimated gamgee, and all the rest of the child's clothing to be kept as scrupulously clean as possible. I further told him to see that a little fresh iodoform was dusted round the stump of the cord until it came off, and the umbilicus was satisfactorily healed.

When Mr Fiddes returned to St Kilda, he commenced battle with the 'knee-woman'. It was long and bitter. But in the end, armed with medical knowledge and antiseptics, he won the day. The centuries-old grip of tetanus infantus on St Kilda was loosened for the short time which remained to the community to enjoy life on their island before they left it for ever. Perhaps Fiddes had won a hollow victory.

Ultimately St Kilda was provided with official medical services which were, inevitably, a charge on the British nation, the cost being in the region of £300 per annum.

2 ST KILDA: ISLAND ECONOMY

DESPITE the forbidding nature of its environment, the St Kildan community was virtually self-supporting. It provided its own food, clothing, fuel and domestic gear. Until the late nineteenth century the economic bases on which the community was founded were broad enough to be relevant in a contemporary context. The economic and social upheavals which followed the Industrial Revolution during last century eventually so influenced the small island community that the islanders became social anachronisms. Their economic bases became irrelevant, not only to the islanders themselves, but also to those outside the community whose tastes had changed and who ceased to find attraction in the low-standard products of the community, which ultimately had to compete with factory products.

The produce of St Kilda over the centuries included cattle, cheese, tweed cloth, blankets, fulmar oil, tallow, wool, feathers, fish (salted cod and ling), sheepskins and knitwear. Rents were paid mostly in cloth and feathers, these items being easily converted into cash by the factor on the mainland. The value of the island's produce was, however, small. In 1875, John Sands, MP and journalist, visited St Kilda and produced a breakdown of the island's exports: cattle—20 head; cheese—918 lb; cloth—227 yd (of 49 in); blankets—403 yd (of 49 in); fulmar oil—566 gall; tallow—414 lb; wool—no quantity given, though some exported; black feathers—2,103 lb; grey feathers—1,675 lb; fish—1,080. The total value was about £250. The price paid to the islanders was only £3 per head. While the economy of the island existed on a non-cash basis, money was not important. But as the St Kildans became more sophisticated, their new requirements resulted in an exports/imports imbalance which the island economy was unable to rectify. The main imports latterly included tea, whisky, meal, sugar, salt, paraffin, metal tools,

Page 71 North Rona: *(above)* ship lying in Geodha a' Stoth, Fianuis; *(below)* the west cliffs in a force 9 gale

Page 72 North Rona: *(above)* the west cliffs; *(below)* guillemots

tobacco, hardware, and simple items of furniture which the islanders could not make for themselves.

The community's primary function—apart from survival—was always to yield sufficient produce to pay for the rent of the island. In 1758 it was £11; by 1883 it had increased to about £95; in 1887 it was about £60, by virtue of new agreements with the owner. The rent was ever a problem and sometimes a source of complaint: at least once in the history of the island the community rebelled against the impositions placed on them by the factor. But by 1928, MacLeod of MacLeod, the owner of St Kilda, had to graciously waive thirteen years of unpaid rent owed to him by the 37 inhabitants remaining on the island two years before their evacuation.

There were, however, times when it seemed that the sun smiled on the community: the bird harvests were good, island produce was exchanged for cash and merchandise and life was good. The following summarises the main items (with typical prices) in the island's economy at various dates:

Prices of Imports 1877

Meal	25s (£1·25) per boll	Leather (soles) 2s (10p) per lb
Oats	25s (£1·25) per boll	Leather (uppers) 2s 3d (11p) per lb
Salt	3s (15p) per cwt	Bonnets (for men) 4s (20p) each
Coarse sugar	7d (3p) per lb	Cravats 3s (15p) each
Tea	5s (25p) per lb	From tourists 5s (25p) per head
Whisky	4s (20p) per bottle	
Tobacco	5s (25p) per lb	

Prices of Exports 1799–1902

1799	A sheep	3s 6d (17·50p)
	A cow	30s (£1·50)
	Feathers	3s (15p) per stone
		sold in the Hebrides for 10s (50p) per stone
1831	A cow	25s 6d (£1·27)
	A pony	25s (£1·25)
1842	Feathers	5s (25p) per stone
		sold on the Scottish mainland for 15s (75p) per stone
1875	A cow	£3
	Tallow	6s 6d (32·5p) per stone
	Cheese	6s (30p) per stone

	Ling	7d (3p) each
	Cod	3d (1p) each
	Bream	1d (½p) each
	Black feathers	6s (30p) per stone
	Grey feathers	5s (25p) per stone
	Fulmar oil	5s (25p) per pint
1877	Cheese	6s 6d (32½p) per stone
1885	Tweed cloth	3s (15p) per yell
	Blanketing	2s 6d (12½p) per yell
1902	Fulmar oil	6d (2½p) per pint
		later 4½d (2p) per pint

St Kilda stone = 24 English lb
St Kilda pint = 5 English pints

BIRDS

The wealth of St Kilda lay undoubtedly in the seabirds which bred in their millions on the high cliffs of the island group. The continued existence of the island community almost wholly depended on the gannet, the fulmar, the puffin, and, to a much lesser extent, on other bird species. The birds were at once a source of food, of produce for export and of basic materials for domestic use.

The gannet (or solan goose) was the foundation of the island's economy. It is a large bird measuring up to 5 ft across the wings when fully spread. Excepting the head, which is brown, and the black tops on the wings, the bird is all white. The bill is long and straight, and has a slight crook at the point. The gannet's egg is slightly less in size than that of the land goose. The main food is the herring and the mackerel. In 1697, when Martin Martin visited St Kilda, gannets formed the principal food. He recorded that 22,600 gannets had been caught in 1696, though this figure has been questioned. Even now, after years of freedom from persecution, the great gannetry at St Kilda is estimated to contain only about 17,000 breeding pairs.

Said Martin:

> We shall take it for granted that there are 100,000 of that kind (solan goose) around the rocks of St Kilda; and this calculation is by far too moderate, as no less than 20,000 of this kind are destroyed every year, including the young ones. We

shall suppose, at the same time, that the solan geese sojourn in these seas for about seven months of the year; that each of them destroys five herrings in a day; a subsistence infinitely poor for so greedy a creature, unless it were more than half supported at the expense of other fishes. Here we have 100,000,000 of the finest fish in the world devoured annually by a single species of the St Kilda sea-fowls.

In 1841, James Wilson estimated that the gannetry at St Kilda, which is still the world's largest, consumed about 300,000 barrels of fish annually, more than the total produced by all the north-east fishing stations in Scotland at that time.

Throughout the history of St Kilda, at no time until about 1910 did any thought of conservation of stock enter into the islanders' minds. The annual slaughter over the years ended with the inevitable result: the islanders had to resort to killing other seabird species to make up the annual quota required for the survival of the human species on the island and to pay the rent. In 1786 it was recorded that over 1,200 gannets were taken in a single night. During the early nineteenth century, the fulmar became the target for the bird-hunters. Even so, seldom did the annual total of gannets killed fall below some 5,000 birds. By 1841, however, the islanders were killing only about 1,400 gannets; in the twentieth century the number fell to 300 birds killed and preserved each year. The gannet colonies are concentrated on Boreray, Stac an Armin, and Stac Lee.

The fulmar is similar in size to the gull. The plumage of the head, neck, breast and tail is a dull white. The wings and back are slate-grey. The pale yellow bill is very strong. The female of the species lays one egg each season, in mid-May. In early August the young fulmar begins to stretch its wings, a sign which heralded the hunting season. While the bird is being caught, it ejects an evil-smelling oily liquid at its captor. The liquid is amber-coloured and its pungent smell pervades everywhere. Before 1878, this Arctic species bred in British waters only at St Kilda. There was a fairly consistent population at some 21,000 breeding pairs.

When the fulmar took over in importance as the main element in the St Kildan economy, very large numbers were caught. In

1910 the year's catch was 9,600 fulmars, compared with 600 gannets.

The third species of seabird which was of importance to the islanders was the puffin. This bird is about the size of a pigeon. The plumage is black on the back, and red and white about the breast. The legs and feet are red. The beak is marked with red, yellow and grey. The bird has a slightly comic look. The main food is fish fry. The puffin lays its single egg in a burrow; if the egg is stolen or raided by a black-back gull, the puffin will lay a replacement. The present puffin population on St Kilda is about 1,000,000 and it is the most common bird in the island group.

According to the Rev N. MacKenzie (*c* 1834), some 18,000 to 20,000 puffins were killed each year during the hunting season. In 1897, 9,000 birds were killed. In 1928, two years before the island's evacuation, the number preserved for human consumption was in the region of 4,000.

Though other seabirds were caught, in no way did the numbers of these killed approach the figures of the gannet, the fulmar and the puffin.

There was a regular timetable for harvesting the seabirds:

February	Razorbill and guillemot
March	Old solan goose
Summer	Puffins and fulmar
Oct/Nov	Young solan goose

Fowling Techniques

The physiology of the St Kildans was evolved through centuries of rock-climbing. The islanders were short, stocky, very muscular and agile. The bone structure of their ankles was most suited to climbing; their toes had a wide set and were almost prehensile. By a process of natural selection, the community was by and large strong and healthy. Those who perished on the island's rock-cliffs were fated, or were otherwise the victims of genuine accidents.

All climbing was done barefoot, or in coarse socks. It was more a matter of lowering on good ropes than in ascending from below. Generally a fowling party moved together rather than singly over the hunting rocks. In more difficult places one man moved at a time, the slack in the rope being taken up by the others. The man on the rope gave his full attention to the serious business of either snaring the birds with a long noosed rod, or reaching for eggs.

Great importance was attached to the quality of the climbing rope, one of the most treasured possessions of an islander. To lose his rope was tantamount to losing his life, for he would then have lost his living. Climbing ropes were often handed down from father to son as heirlooms. In former times they were made of plaited horsehair (served and parcelled) and even of straw. A good horsehair rope had a life of some fifty years. The material was derived from the island's stock of horses which became largely extinct *c* 1840. In Martin Martin's time there were three ropes on St Kilda, each about 150 ft long and reckoned to have the same value in exchange or barter as two good cows. A new-made rope was tested by putting a strain on it: four men pulling against the weight of a large boulder round which one end of the rope was tied. If the rope passed this test without breaking, it was deemed safe to use for fowling by the island's Parliament. *A' sheachd beannachd nan cairdean 's a lon laidir na feuma* (Sevenfold blessings to the friends and the strong rawhide rope in time of need)—not for nothing did the climbing rope enter into the island's proverbial sayings. Latterly, the ropes were made of Manilla hemp. Another article used for bird-catching was a rod fully 10 ft long with a noose at the end. This was carried in the hand. A clasp-knife was often carried on a string hung round the catcher's neck. In the early years of the community's existence the fowlers went foraging alone. Later, the fowling team usually comprised four men, one of whom fastened the rope end round his chest, low enough to allow maximum freedom of movement. The other end was held securely, without stakes, by those at the cliff head. Fulmars were killed by having their necks broken. A special twist in the neck was necessary to 'lock in' the oil which was the St Kildan's source of light in the dark winter nights. As the fowler killed he threw the birds into a safe place and made his way slowly along the nesting ledges.

After a quantity of birds had been killed, the fowler shouted to his companions who pulled their partner, laden with dead birds (each weighing 2–3 lb) to the cliff top. When the ropes were not long enough to allow the fowler to reach the lowest nesting ledges, a series of ropes and holding teams was established on the cliff face. The fulmar harvest began on 12 August, all fowling ropes having been duly inspected and passed by the Parliament the previous day. The harvest period usually lasted three weeks. The Parliament also decided which parts of the rocks should be cleared of birds, and on which days. All other work was virtually dropped once the bird-catching season arrived. As the poem says: 'Away my spade! and up, my rope and snare, I've heard the gannet on the sea!'

The gannets were to be found only on Boreray and the other St Kildan stacs. They were difficult to obtain, both because of their method of nesting and the patience, time and skill required of the fowlers. In addition, the birds had to be taken at night while they sat on their nests. The sentry bird had to be killed first, otherwise it would cry out and alarm the whole colony. Once this bird was killed, a task requiring patience and skill, the sleeping birds were knocked on the head with a thick stick and thrown down the cliff faces into the sea below where the carcases were picked up by the waiting boat.

The puffins were mostly caught by the women and children on the island, the bird colonies being in the more accessible horizontal cliff-tops rather than on the faces. Puffin-snaring began with a curious rite. A bird was caught and removed of all its feathers except those on the wings and tail. It was then set free when it would be attacked by the other puffins. Says Sands 1875:

> While the sagacious animals (the dogs) pawed at one hole, they (the women) kept a watchful eye on the burrows adjacent as if they expected the puffins to issue from them. Some of the girls at the same time were plunging their hands deep into the holes and dragging out the birds, and twisting their necks with a dexterity which only long practice could give.

Snares were often made of horsehair. The dogs were specially trained to catch puffins.

Harvest Yield

In 1875, Sands reported the yield for that year: fulmar oil—

566 gall; black feathers—2,103 lb; grey feathers—1,675 lb. Some of the oil was exported direct to Skye where it was used for smearing sheep; it was more often sold to the factor. Very few of the puffin carcases were eaten, the puffin being killed mainly for its feathers.

Two bird species were subjected to the communalistic division of spoils: the solan goose and the fulmar. The birds killed were divided equally amongst the islanders. After the division, each share was taken back to the family home where the men, women and children would spend long nights plucking the birds and preparing the carcases for preservation as food during the winter. The feathers were carefully set aside and sorted for sale to the factor. Each fulmar gave a yield of about half a pint of oil, the liquid being squeezed out of the carcase and put into canisters. The carcase was then split lengthways down the back, and the viscera removed to be used for manure. The whole was then salted and stored in special barrels. About 200 birds filled one barrel; each family had about 4 or 5 barrels kept in the cleits.

AGRICULTURE

In 1697 the islanders, according to Martin Martin, gave voice to their lack of desire to extend their agricultural activities; this, even though the soil was sweet and fertile, and the barley produced was the largest in the Western Isles. It ripened earlier than in other parts and was an important item of export from the island. Even by 1819, MacCulloch wrote that the barley '. . . is by much the finest to be seen in the whole circuit of the isles'.

Agriculture was an incidental pursuit and came nowhere near the popularity of bird catching. The abundance and certainty of the sea birds were far more important than reliance on scanty soil, however well it might be cultivated. Agricultural activity was restricted to an area of a few acres below the village. The system of land use was that found in other parts of the Highlands and islands, ie runrig, in which the strips of soil were interchanged every three years. The earliest crops were barley and oats. Later potatoes, cabbages and turnips were grown. Though the soil surface was thin, it was kept well manured by peat ash, bird carcases and the occasional old thatch from a house (well-sooted by the peat fire). The main implement of cultivation was the *cas-chrom* (bent foot) which was essentially a long wooden handle with a right-angled iron socket. Until the year of evacuation (1930) the quern was used to grind the grain.

As much as fifty acres within the township wall were usually cultivated with a few acres lying fallow. By 1927 only two acres were sown with potatoes and corn. The remaining area produced luxuriant bracken, dockens and other weeds.

But even with good cropping techniques there could be the occasional famine. In July of 1841 J. Wilson found:

> The people are suffering very much from want of food. During spring, ere the birds came, they literally cleared the shore, not only of shell-fish, but even of a species of sea-weed that grows abundantly on the rocks within the sea-mark. For a time then they were better off, particularly as long as fresh eggs could be got. Now the weather is coarse, birds cannot be found, at least in such abundance as their needs require. Sorrel boiled in water is the principal part of the food of some, and even that grass is getting scarce. All that was near is exhausted, and they go to the rocks for it, where formerly they used to go for birds only.

That old standby, and latterly the staff of life for the Highlander, the potato, was not cultivated in St Kilda to the extent it was in other parts of the Highlands. It was estimated in 1877 that a barrel of potatoes weighing about 220 lb would hardly yield an extra 100 lb from the sowing. Not only was the yield small in number, but those potatoes which did manage to survive the growing season were soft and tasted like yams when lifted, because of the effects of the sea spray which often enveloped the island in a salt-tasting cloud of mist.

Oats were sown thickly: about 12 bushels per acre. The yield was rarely above three times the amount planted. About the year 1877 it was discovered that the seed corn used by the islanders had not been changed for some sixty years and the crop yield, and the seed strain, had greatly deteriorated.

The islanders were more progressive and productive in animal husbandry than in the cultivation of their land. The arable land of the island was shared out equally among the families, the division being carried out by the Parliament. The head of each household was responsible for about one and a half acres of land, though this amount has fluctuated through the centuries. When Lord Brougham saw St Kilda (1799) he wrote of Village Bay, 'The great bosom is divided into 400 rips, or fields of barley and oats and potatoes—25 feet by three!'

Robert Connell, reporting back to the *Glasgow Herald* in 1887 wrote:

> The total area of arable land has been estimated at 40 acres which would give an average of 2½ acres per croft . . . For house and croft the rent is £2 per annum . . . Over and above this £2, the people pay rent for the common pasture of the island. For the grazing of each cow the charge made by the proprietor is 7s per annum. For sheep, the charge is 9d a head on St Kilda and 6d a head on the adjacent islands. By no manner of means can it be held that these rates are excessive. The total rental of the island in 1885–6 was about £60, but before any reader fetches his slate to find out what rate of interest this represents on a capital sum of £3000—the price paid by the present proprietor in 1871—let me hasten to explain that not a penny of it went into the pocket of MacLeod. The expenses of factorship, which are necessarily heavy, including, as they do, two trips to the island every year in a smack specially chartered for the purpose, would appear to have eaten up all that the crofters saw their way to pay. Of course, the people could hardly be crofters if they were not in arrears to the landlord.
>
> Formerly the islanders paid each year on a fixed number of sheep and cattle. Some were possibly paying too much and others too little. The people regarding this method of fixing the rents as a grievance, and at their request the proprietor lately agreed to regulate the rent each year by the actual number of cattle and sheep in the possession of the islanders . . . The number of cattle on the island was ascertained to be about 40, and of sheep the total number on St Kilda and adjacent islands was close upon 1,000 . . . The cattle are of the West Highland breed, mostly black, or red and black, in colour. A considerable proportion of the sheep are of the old St Kilda breed; the others are a cross between that and the blackfaced variety.

The St Kildan livestock has been counted at various times. The following summary table is taken from O'Dell and Walton *The Highlands and Islands of Scotland*:

Year	*Sheep*			*Cattle*	*Horses*
	Total	On Soay	On Boreray		
1697	2,000	500	400	98	18
1758	1,000	500	400	40	10
1824	1,000	4/500	4/500	90	
1841	2,000	500	400		2/3
1861	1,500	300	500	43	—
1875	1,200/ 1,500	400		50	
1883		200			—
1927		400	400		—
1930				14	—

Note: — means None; a blank means No mention.

The cattle were kept, in the old-type houses, in the partitioned-off section of the building. Goats were once common on St Kilda, but were removed from the island in the nineteenth century because they disturbed the more valuable nesting birds. The horses were used to carry peats and were a good source of manure. They were cleared from the island in the early 1840s because it was said that they damaged the pastures. One result of their evacuation was the removal of good turf from many hundreds of useful acres near the township to serve as fuel. Previously the horses had carried the turf from a farther distance; lacking the horses' backs, the islanders preferred to spare their own and cut their turf nearer to the house. In Martin's time there were 18 horses, small red-coloured ponies imported from the mainland. In 1697, some 100 cows on the island were small, fat and sweet-fleshed. Though the number fluctuated over the centuries they were always important for their by-products. If the islands had pursued an efficient land-use policy over the years, they could well have maintained an enviable agrarian economy and perhaps by 1930 at least there would have been no great need for evacuation.

FISHING

The Dutch, in the seventeenth century, were the first active fishers in the waters of the western seas around St Kilda. Realising the great potential to be harvested, they prosecuted the activity with such vigour that one wonders why their example was rarely followed by the islanders of the Hebrides themselves. Though the sea was in the islanders' blood, derived largely from the Norse element in their forebears, it was to roam as emigrants rather than to fish that they looked to the sea.

Fishing as an economic activity in St Kilda was followed more often than not simply to introduce a dietary change. The island's boats were used more as a communications link with the Hebrides and to convey the bird-catchers to St Kilda's satellite island rocks. It was not until 1875 that fish as an element in the island's economic make-up was sufficiently important to be enumerated. Angling from the island's rocks was prohibited, otherwise the birds would be disturbed and they were more important. One reason given for the islanders' lack of interest in fishing was their belief that too much fish in the diet resulted in skin eruptions, though this did not deter the islanders from accepting, in the latter years of the nineteenth century, substantial gifts of fish from trawlers sheltering in the haven of Village Bay. In the 1870s, only two boats were occupied in fishing; the cod and ling caught were salted for sale to the factor. These two species, *inter alia*, abounded in the waters round the island group.

Robert Connell, writing after his visits in 1885–7, said after proposing the construction of a suitable harbour:

> With such a harbour as is proposed, and with the four boats they presently have, the people would be able to add largely to their wealth, for unquestionably the waters around their island abound with cod, ling and other fish. Moreover, if the island became a fishing station, it would be more regularly visited by steamers, attracted by the prospects of freights, and the grievance so much complained of, that the islanders in the matter of buying and selling are entirely at the mercy of the factor who makes his own prices, would speedily be removed. It is notorious, however, that the St Kildans are bad sailors and

fishermen, and it is doubtful whether a boat harbour would be of much real practical value after all, unless indeed a number of practical fishermen from the East or West Coast could be induced to take up their abode on the island and impart their training and experience to the natives.

In 1819, MacCulloch remarked that the islanders' lack of interest in fishing was due to their ability to obtain wealth from other occupations, especially fowling: 'They possess already as much food as they can consume and are under no temptation to augment it by another perilous and laborious employment.'

In most instances, when fish were caught, their livers were retained and the remainder, except for a few saved for curing, thrown to the dogs. The livers were used as a source of food (fish-heads were stuffed with them to make a dish called *ceann-cropic*). They were also a source of oil for medicinal and lighting purposes.

In 1860, the captain of the *Porcupine* carried off St Kilda some 16 cwt of fish which the islanders had caught. He returned with £16. A return on such a scale inspired some young men. But when they considered the fickle seas around them, and their slender boats, they gave up the idea of fishing as an occupation.

By 1902, the islanders were supplanting seabirds with substantial amounts of fish in their diet. What they caught was for their own consumption; little was cured for export.

DOMESTIC ECONOMY

John Sands first visited St Kilda in 1875 and subsequently presented a paper on the island's antiquity to the Society of Antiquaries of Scotland. He writes:

As some of the existing manners and customs of the St Kildans may throw a light upon the habits of ancient and primitive populations, I shall try to describe them. The ground is now all dug with the spade, but I saw a *cass chrom* or two put away on the rafters of barns. A wooden rake is used instead of a harrow. Oats, bere, and potatoes, and a few cabbages and turnips. Reaping hooks are sometimes used to cut the crop, but in general it is pulled up by the roots, the straw being used to thatch old houses and cellars. The grain is thrashed out with a flail. It is scorched in a pot or put into a straw tub (like a flat-topped bee-hive), and dried with heated stones. It is then ground by hand-mills. The women sit on the ground half-naked, and work at the mill like furies. Sheepskins, stretched on a hoop and perforated with a hot wire, serve as sieves. . . . The meal is baked into cakes and made into gruel and porridge. Meat is often cooked along with these . . .

Lucifer matches, although used by the minister, are looked upon as curiosities by the people, who smile when one is struck. Nor is there a flint and steel on the island. The turf fires are always kept burning, and if one happens to go out a live turf is borrowed from a neighbour. When parties of men or women go to the adjacent islands they take a kettle of burning turf with them. If the embers are covered with turf and ashes the fire will survive for a great many hours. I myself had no matches, and never required to borrow a cinder for some months. The fires in St Kilda have probably been burning for centuries.

According to Robert Connell (1887), the diet of the St Kildans was:

Breakfast	Porridge and milk, with the flesh of the fulmar afterwards occasionally, the bird being boiled in the porridge.
Dinner	Mutton, or the flesh of the fulmar or solan goose, with potatoes when there are any.
Tea	Tea and bread and cheese, the flesh of the fulmar occasionally, and sometimes porridge.

The islanders take breakfast between nine and ten; dinner generally not till about four, and sometimes an hour or two later, on their return from the rocks or the fields; and tea about nine in summer, and as late as eleven in winter, when they sit up at their looms till about two in the morning. There is a complete absence of variety in their food. This, along with the lack of fresh vegetables and the indigestible nature of the flesh of the birds which they eat, is a frequent cause of dyspepsia, from which many of the islanders suffer.

Milk and sea-bird's eggs are consumed in considerable quantities during the summer; tea, sugar, and flour are now used in nearly every house; potatoes are the only vegetables pro-

> curable—the quantity grown on the island is small and the quality bad, and the supply is only available usually for six months. It therefore follows that the dietary of the people is practically devoid of vegetables for the half of each year. Such condiments as vinegar, pepper, mustard, and pickles are not used. Whisky is relished very much, and every man keeps his bottle, but nobody drinks to excess. On the whole, the people live well; all that is wanted is a greater variety and more vegetable food. A Skyeman, who had been often on the island for various lengths of time, gave me his opinion in these terms—'They are the best fed people in creation. I speak the truth, master.'

Latterly, in the twentieth century, there was little to distinguish the St Kildan from other Highlanders, at first sight. Only in their insularity were they different. Otherwise they had the same trappings as had similar communities in the Highlands and Islands. In many respects, the island community was better off than the latter for it had a ample supply of food both from birds and from the fish around the coast. But, like the Irish in the Hungry Forties, the islanders did not use these resources. Instead they suffered privation.

TOURISM

In much the same way as travellers in the eighteenth and nineteenth centuries made the Grand Tour of Europe to broaden their education, towards the end of the nineteenth century their tours included St Kilda, on the edge of the known world. As much an adventure as an African safari, an actual voyage to St Kilda was regarded as necessary to fill the gap between imagination and hard fact concerning the island and its people. This interest in the island was often excited by the writings of past visitors: Martin Martin, the ministers Buchan and MacAulay, Lord Brougham, John MacCulloch and others. Perhaps because he was the island's first recorder, and because he had first-hand knowledge, Martin was favourite reading; many of the island's features, such as the wells of the Lover's Stone (see page 56), were nothing if not excellent guide-book material.

The first steam-boat visited the island in 1834. The islanders rushed to tell the minister that a ship on fire was approaching St Kilda. In 1838 the *Vulcan* dropped anchor in Village Bay on Saturday 28 July. Said a visitor in a letter home: 'I am at length, thank God, arrived on terra firma in St Kilda, the place which, of all other places within the British dominions, I longed most to see; and I had not certainly been led to form a false or exaggerated conception on it; nay, the half had not been told me.' The *Vulcan* fired a large cannon to herald her safe arrival. 'The natives were seen running down Aois-mheall like a flock of goats running for their lives—all bare-headed, bare-footed and coats off.' In time, the islanders became all too familiar with the steady stream of ships of all kinds.

It was not until 1877 that the island's tourist trade really began. Before that date visitors to St Kilda were of a better breed than the tourists bent on satisfying idle curiosity. In 1877, the 240 ton SS *Dunara Castle* was advertised as offering a voyage to the 'romantic Western Isles and lone St Kilda'. The fare was £10 for the 10-day voyage taken in cabin-class comfort with full board. Some forty passengers took up the offer and found themselves in Village Bay on the morning of 2 July. 'After breakfasting on board the *Dunara*, the passengers began to land in detachments about half-past nine. Heavy rain fell during breakfast; but the weather speedily improved, and the sun shone forth most auspiciously.' The natives co-operated: '. . . uttering a shrill Gaelic cry, he descended barefoot, skipping and singing as he went, and occasionally standing out nearly at a right angle from the beetling cliff!'

Other ships followed the *Dunara Castle*, including the *Lady Ambrosine* and the *Hebridean*, both of which belonged to Martin Orme. Ships under the flag of McCallum, Orme & Co Ltd, sailed the Hebridean seas fulfilling both a social and a commercial function, as did the vessels of MacBraynes Ltd who absorbed them in 1948. In 1898 the *Hebridean* was replaced by the SS *Hebrides* and from then on both she and the *Dunara Castle* plied the Hebridean waters during the summer months until 1939. In 1885, when the islanders experienced a disaster brought on by a great storm, it was the *Hebridean* which was chartered to make a special trip to St Kilda with freight worth £110, including seed corn, barley, meal and potatoes.

It is ironic that the *Dunara Castle*, which began the tourist trade that is said to have started the rot in St Kilda, took part in the evacuation of the island in 1930. The ship was broken up in the summer of 1948. Occasionally other well-known west Highland ships, such as the ss *Clydesdale*, called at St Kilda.

Tourists fell into two groups. First there was the professional group which included sociologists, naturalists, doctors and the like; for the most part they either camped on the island or lodged in island homes. The other group contained the curious, who regarded the islanders as elements in a human menagerie and preferred their more comfortable ship's base to living ashore. But the tourist, whatever the type, played an undoubted part in the buoyancy of the island's economy. They bought much of the island's produce (tweeds, knitwear, sheepskins, and other articles of St Kildan manufacture).

The general tourist brought evil in his wake. Wrote Connell in 1886: 'One cannot be long on the island without discovering the great moral injury that tourists and sentimentalists and yachtsmen, with pocketsful of money, are working upon a kindly community and simple people.'

The introduction of a cash economy into the island was in some ways timely. Paying rent in kind rather than in cash had become an economic anachronism and the St Kildan was, one feels, glad that the tourist brought money to be exchanged for the island's products. This money allowed the islanders to participate in the national economic system. With money, they were able to buy direct—grain and foodstuffs, clothing, articles of furniture, and the occasional bottle of spirits, not to mention the large quantities of tobacco of which the islanders had become more than fond during the previous century or so.

Alexander Ross wrote in 1884:

> By the frequent visits of tourists and yachtsmen, and the liberal gifts of wine and clothes of the latest fashion, the St Kildan has ceased to be the unsophisticated mortal he was 30 years ago, and though by no means spoiled or importunate in his demands, he is, I believe degenerating like some other of

Page 89: (above) Seal in sea pool on North Rona; *(below)* young gannets on Sulasgeir

Page 90 Sulasgeir: *(above)* approach from the west; *(below)* all stores must be hauled up from the small boat to the top of the cliffs

the Highlanders, and is not ashamed to accept gifts, if not to beg them.

The tourist season was the islanders' silly season. John Ross (1889) wrote:

> The excitement caused by the entrance of one steamer occupies the minds of the natives until the approach of another. And while excited they are incapable of doing anything but talking of what they have seen and heard . . . The St Kildans are spoiled children. This is the only opportunity afforded them of 'turning a penny' and they are just over-pressing in taking advantage of it. A few years back, visitors there used to scatter money right and left, and the poor natives expect that it should run a little more freely now.

The day following each visit was reserved for the sole purpose of discussing the visitors, their scale of generosity, the prices obtained in hard bargaining, and 'incidents'.

Inevitably, the way of life of the islanders changed. In particular, the islander began to rely too much on regular communication with the mainland, when for centuries his forebears had been content with an annual visit from the factor. The changed conditions introduced psychological upsets and made for the acceptance in the late 1920s of the need for emigration to solve their problems. More than money caused this situation. The St Kildans knew that they were regarded as human freaks. Wrote Norman Heathcote in 1900:

> I do not wonder that they dislike foreigners, as so many tourists treat them as if they were wild animals at the Zoo . . . I have seen them (the tourists) standing at the church door during service laughing and talking, and staring in as if at an entertainment got up for their amusement.

The attitude of such sight-seers was undoubtedly resented by the St Kildan, and it is not to be wondered that the islanders sought to fleece the gawpers who landed on their shores. In the process they got the name of being rather greedy. Rather it was the only way in which the islanders could retaliate for the tourists' imposition on their community of a situation which could do nothing but get out of hand. Unable to adapt to the standards set by society, the islanders eventually failed both themselves and their island home.

CLOTH-MAKING

In common with many other Highland and island communities, the St Kildans were self-sufficient in their clothing needs, only looking to external sources for finery and gee-gaws which the island's own resources could not provide. The cloth made was a heavy coarse type, suited to the simple needs of the islanders but never a particularly attractive item for general purchase by an external market. Inevitably, the methods used in making the cloth were primitive. John Sands wrote in 1875:

> The sheep are plucked, sheep-shears being unknown. The wool is spun by the wheel into thread for cloth, blankets and stockings. Thread for sewing is spun by the spindle and distaff. The women dye the thread with indigo (bought from the factor), and with lichen found on stones. Almost every man is a weaver in winter. The looms are all made of wood without any iron. The cloth they make is all twilled, which requires four treadles.

An earlier report (*c* 1727) tells of the manner in which the islanders fulled, thickened or waulked their cloth. They

> . . . thicken their cloth upon stakes or rods or mats of hay twisted or woven together in small ropes; they worked hard at this employment, first making use of their hands and at last their feet; and when they are at work they commonly sing all the time, one of their number acting the part of a prime chantress, whom all the rest follow and obey.

Cloth, as a major item of export, did not appear until about 1850. At about this time, the cloth which was to become known as Harris Tweed was gaining an increasing reputation in the markets in London. St Kilda tweed, a cloth of similar texture, was associated in people's minds with the Harris cloth and its characteristic qualities were appreciated in similar markets. The wool for the cloth came from the plucked domesticated and wild Soay sheep. The women folk spun it into yarn; the men wove the yarn into cloth. In 1879 there were thirty-six spinning wheels on St Kilda. Every house possessed a loom, made from wood supplied by the proprietor of the island. The exported cloth was twilled and of a natural colour. In attempts to dye the wool, failure occurred more often than success and the indifferent results spoiled the cloth. In the end, the factor preferred to buy the cloth in its natural state for subsequent sale and processing on the Scottish mainland.

The cloth, though coarse and rough in character, was held in high regard by the appreciative few; the romantic aura already growing about the island helped its ready sale. Much of it was sold in Stornoway, Lewis, where it was often made into suitings. In 1892 a St Kildan, Alexander Ferguson, emigrated to Glasgow where he set up a successful business as a tweed merchant handling, among other cloths, St Kilda tweed which was in fair demand.

The islanders were paid about 3s (15p) per *yell* or 'big yard' of tweed cloth *c* 1885. A yell was an old Scots measure defined as 47 inches and a thumb. Later the more reasonable yard of 36 in was introduced and the island's weavers reaped a more appropriate reward for their labours. In 1914, Professor W. R. Scott, who occupied the Adam Smith Chair of Political Economy at Glasgow University, presented his *Report to the Board of Agriculture for Scotland on Home industries in the Highlands and Islands.* It contains much interesting information about craft industries and tweed, as produced in St Kilda and the other Hebridean islands. The following is an extract from an Appendix in the Report on the earnings of labour expended in making St Kilda tweeds carded by hand:

> . . . a man and his wife working together would make a web of St Kilda tweed of 30 yards in 5 weeks. The woman works 12 hours a day, that is, 360 hours, while the man does all the weaving (which takes 48 hours), and helps in the teasing and carding . . . the wool being valued at a lower rate, being taken at only 9d per lb. Thus, the St Kilda earnings would be approximately 1¾d per hour.

With the increase in the numbers of tourists visiting St Kilda, cloth became an important item of island produce offered for on-the-spot sales, and for export. By 1928, some 1,200 yd of tweed were being exported annually. This was about the only manufactured article which the islanders had to give in exchange for the various commodities they required. But the ascendancy of Harris Tweed in the Hebrides, being cheaper, and better in quality and range of shades and designs, went against the St Kildan product. This factor, coupled with the high cost of transportation to the Scottish mainland, resulted in St Kilda tweed being unable to find a place in a highly competitive market. In addition, the market was fickle: purchasers bought the product only because of its association with the island and not always for its qualities as a cloth.

The islanders found themselves in a cleft stick. If the island's factor was instructed to sell the cloth to a larger and less discriminative market, the reduced sale price would yield little or no return for the labour in making the cloth. On the other hand, to make the cloth more cheaply would incur great expense in introducing near-factory facilities to produce a cloth which could compete with the material being made in large quantities from mill-supported methods in the Western Isles. The decline in the demand for St Kilda tweed was one of the contributing factors in the final decision to evacuate the island. The disappearance of an important element in the economy of any community leads to a drastic stock-taking; if there are no alternatives to fill the gap, desertion is the only remedy. An economic yardstick was applied to the island and its community which failed to measure up to it. Perhaps had a social yardstick been applied, and had society made an effort to appreciate the validity of the St Kildans' desire to remain a social entity, the ultimate desertion of the island might well have been delayed, if not put off altogether.

COMMUNICATIONS

On 24 September 1885, a local resident of Aird Uig, a township on the west coast of Lewis, picked up off the beach a small piece of wood, fashioned like a boat and rigged with a tiny mast and sail. Tied to the wood was a bottle containing a letter, written on a page from a school exercise book. It was addressed to Mr

Kenneth Campbell, teacher, Uig, Lewis, by Stornoway. The message was:

> My dear Sir—I am now going to write you a letter and sending her in one of the little ships in which we were sailing on the shore as you know to let you know all the knews. the men were building a house just a little house for the cows a great storm came on and all the corn and barley were swept away by the storm and one of the boats was swept away by the sea the men of St Kilda is nearly dead with the hunger. They send two boats from St Kilda to go to Haries (Harris) not the fishing boats but little piece of wood like the little one which I send. I sent my best loves unto you—I am yours truly, Alexander Ferguson.

In this way did the St Kildan community keep in touch with the Hebridean islands to the east. Occasionally messages were put in bottles. More often messages were sent tied to a piece of wood and attached to a round buoy (sheepskin floats) with a little red flag. It was then left to the currents of the Atlantic Ocean and the westerlies to push the St Kildan post off the island to find its way to western shores (often as far distant as the Orkneys) where it would be picked up. Although communications were always primitive, it was not until the late nineteenth century that their efficiency was called into question. The islanders began to rely on them increasingly to convey messages of recurring distress; time therefore became important.

But even when steamships became common at St Kilda, communications were poor. About twice each year, the proprietor sent a vessel; touring yachts and steamers called occasionally, but mostly in the summer months. The mails came to the island six times a year in 1883, though some eight months could pass between one call and the next. In the twentieth century it was the Aberdeen and other trawlers which conveyed messages to and from the island.

In 1877, the GPO established formal postal communications with Fair Isle and immediately the same service was requested for St Kilda. But the Fair Isle service was provided as an *en route* facility from steamers plying between Aberdeen and the Shetland Islands. St Kilda was *en route* to nowhere. In 1879 a proposal that the island's factor, John MacKenzie, should be subsidised to carry mails to the island failed. Eventually an arrangement was made by the GPO and various tourist steamers calling at St Kilda to deliver and collect mails; but most of the activity was concentrated during the three months of summer. In 1898, recognising the service given to the islanders by the Aberdeen trawlers in particular, a further arrangement was made by the GPO that all mail for St Kilda was to be sent through Aberdeen. The Post Office, however, failed to mention suitable recompense for the trawlermen and the service depended wholly on the goodwill of the fishermen from Aberdeen who fished in the St Kildan waters. Any mail from St Kilda was given to the trawlermen, with money for postage stamps, to be posted at Aberdeen.

Towards the end of 1899 it was proposed by the factor that a sub-Post Office be established on St Kilda, to remain open all the year round. The first official St Kilda Post Office came into being on 20 September 1899. It was set up in a room of the factor's house on the island. The following year the minister, Rev Angus Fiddes, was appointed sub-postmaster at £5 per annum plus bonuses. The island's clerics held the post until 1905 when Neil Ferguson became the first native, and the last, to take over the work, which he did until 1930. Formal recognition by the GPO never overcame the main problem of carrying mails to and from St Kilda all the year round on a regular basis.

In 1968 the National Trust for Scotland produced a set of St Kilda stamps, more correctly called local carriage labels and similar to the local labels produced for some small Scottish islands. The stamps are used for prepaying postage on mail carried between St Kilda and the Hebrides or the Scottish mainland. The stamps depict the bird life for which the islands are famous. The 4d stamp shows a great auk, commemorating one of the last sightings of the now-extinct species on Stac an Armin some 130 years previously. The other stamps depict the St Kilda wren, gannet, shag, guillemot, kittiwake, puffin and Leach's fork-tailed petrel.

The St Kilda set of labels is the work of Miss Jennifer Toombs who designed the Churchill Omnibus Series for the British Crown Colonies and the Churchill sets for British Guinea, Gambia and

Jamaica. The labels are the first of a series being issued to publicise the work of the National Trust as well as the interesting birds and flowers of St Kilda. Only those going to St Kilda on working parties organised by the National Trust, or on one of the cruises run by the Trust with calls at St Kilda, will have the labels franked with a special cancelling date stamp. The old original postmarks are much sought after by collectors, as they are rare relics of an island community now no longer existing. The income derived from the sale of the St Kilda stamps is being used for the benefit of the working parties and other groups who visit St Kilda each year to do nature research and to maintain the relics of the once-thriving St Kildan population.

The maintenance of communications, so long as time was not important, was of small value to the islanders. What was more important to them was a way of contacting the outside world in times of urgent need. The matter was brought to a head when the community faced starvation in 1912 and it was a trawler which brought the news to the mainland. The news was given nationwide prominence and the *Daily Mirror* organised a relief expedition. 'Dear Editor,' wrote the thankful islanders, 'a thousand thanks for your great kindness to the lonely St Kildans in their distress for the want of provisions. Your help reached us unexpectedly, and left us more than thankful for it.'

It was due to the generosity of H. Gordon Selfridge, the London stores owner, that the island was to have its own wireless transmitter. The proprietor of St Kilda readily gave permission for the station to be erected and the Postmaster General granted a license. Work was put in hand but was brought to a sudden stop. Another trawler reached the mainland with the news that the whole community was ill with influenza. Again a relief mission went to St Kilda. The wireless transmitting station was completed on 22 July 1913 and the local missionary was instructed in its use. But the equipment broke down soon afterwards and it was not until the 1914–18 War that it became operational again as a War Signal Station.

But it was destined to be short-lived. On 18 May 1918, the station attracted the attention of a German submarine and did not survive the shelling.

PIER FACILITIES

It was not until 1902 that the island was finally provided with a pier. Before this date passengers landing on the island from visiting ships had to be ferried across Village Bay to the shore. The pier, made from concrete, had steps and an iron ladder on its western side. It projected from the shore on the northern side of Village Bay just westward of the manse. It protected a boat slip situated between it and the shore. The pier was normally accessible to boats, except when a full gale was blowing. It was somewhat useless at low water owing to thick seaweed growths and heavy boulders on the sea bottom in the vicinity of the pier.

In 1969, two copies of *The Scotsman* newspaper, dated October 1899, were found in some packages in the old jetty partly demolished during work by military personnel to lengthen and strengthen it.

3 ST KILDA: ISLAND HISTORY

THE early history of St Kilda is obscure. For centuries, the island community kept no records to preserve for succeeding generations the interesting events which went hand in hand with the evolution of the island society. In 1697 the St Kildans were amazed that Martin Martin could record speech and express himself in writing. Writing may have been an unnecessary activity on the island, but even the tradition of transmitting history orally, as was common on the Scottish mainland, in the Western Isles, and in Ireland, does not seem to have been followed; otherwise we should have today much of the island's oral tradition fixed in perpetuity by the transcripts of visitors to St Kilda during the eighteenth and nineteenth centuries.

It can be assumed that the islands have been occupied, though not necessarily continuously, for between 1,000 and 2,000 years. Excavations on the main island of Hirt have revealed an earth-house of the Iron Age type; and in Gleann Mor, the plan of a group of circular (multiple) huts looks archaic but the date is uncertain. Though the earth-house and semi-underground structures were very common throughout the Western Isles until about a century ago, they are accepted as forms of construction which are eminently suitable to the climate of these parts and have an extremely long lineage. On Dun there are the remains of a hill-fort, from which 'dun' is probably derived. Many writers have commented on the St Kildan's disrespect for antiquity. Any ready supply of building material was removed without a second thought, with the result that much of antiquarian interest has been lost. Martin Martin mentions three churches. Today their sites are known but little remains of the original structures. The churches were Christ Church, St Brendan's and St Columba's.

It is reasonable to suppose that in prehistoric times St Kilda was occupied by a settlement in Gleann Mor located on the side of the island opposite to Village Bay. This is thought to be the first settlement on the island. What caused this settlement to cease its existence and the new Village Bay community to come into being is not known. It could be attributable to many factors: change of climate; change in land use; increased interest in sea-birds as a source of food and item of exchange and barter; and the greater degree of accessibility afforded by Village Bay. The theory that the original settlement was wiped out by disease or Norse invader is also reasonable and Village Bay may in fact have seen the establishment of a new society by an invader to whom a maritime environment was familiar. The influence of the Norse during the eighth and subsequent centuries on the west coast of Scotland and in the Hebrides may well have reached St Kilda.

The present settlement site in Village Bay dates from *c* 1830. Before this date the settlement was nearer the beach. The earlier community seems to have been concentrated around the spring called *Tobar Childa*, meaning Kilda's Well. This well was 'near the heart of the village, and is of universal use to the community'.

Some of what are now called 'cleits' around this well were once built to serve as dwellings. This is apparent in their structure and design, both aspects being different from the many cleits or store-houses built as such. They are broader and have a greater headroom.

The Settlement of Gleann Mor

The prehistoric settlement of Gleann Mor, or Glen Bay, is in a fine U-shaped valley. Stone monuments of obvious antiquity litter the area, once the dwelling-place of a pastoral community. The structure which is of greatest interest is the 'Amazon's House' *(tigh na banaghaisgich)*. Martin Martin first recorded the building in 1697. But it was not until 1957 that it was realised this beehive structure was only a small part of the extensive Gleann Mor settlement. F. W. Thomas, in a paper to the Society of Antiquaries of Scotland in 1862, described the house. However, Martin's description (1697) is the more picturesque:

> Upon the west side of the Isle lies a Valley, with a Declination towards the Sea, with a Rivulet running through the middle of it, on each side of which is an Ascent of half a Mile; all which

Piece of Ground is called by the inhabitants, The Female Warrior's Glen: This Amazon is famous in their Traditions: Her House or Dairy of Stone is yet extant . . . and is in the form of a Circle Pyramid-wise towards the Top with a Vent in it, the Fire being always in the Centre of the Floor . . . The Body of this House contains not above Nine Persons sitting; there are three Beds, or low Vaults at the side of the wall, which contains Five Men each, and are separated by a Pillar; at each Entry to one of these low Vaults is a Stone standing upon one end; upon this she is reported ordinarily to have laid her Helmet; there are two Stones on the other side, upon which she is said to have laid her Sword: they tell you that she was much addicted to Hunting, and that in her Days all the Space betwixt this Isle and that of Harries (Harris), was one continued Tract of Dry Land.

Martin himself coined the phrase 'Amazon's House'. The translation of the Gaelic is 'Female Warrior's House'. One wonders whether this ancient St Kildan community was one with a matriarchal system of government.

Another beehive dwelling is Calum Mor's house. It stands north of the graveyard and close to Kilda's Well. It contains some very large blocks of stone, some of them weighing half a ton. Inside, the house measures 14′ x 7′ and is half underground.

There are sixteen structures in the glen which conform to a definite type, though they differ both in size and constructional details. Each is approached between curved or horned walls of dry-stone which converge on the narrow gateway of a small open courtyard. Around the court are clustered, in clover-leaf fashion, a few beehive-shaped chambers. They are skilfully corbelled towards the top and are finished off with a few broad lintels, the whole being originally roofed with turf. Some chambers have recesses in the walls. Many of the older cleits in Village Bay and clustered around Tobar Childa display this form of constructional detail, particularly the technique of corbelling inwards to a ceiling of slabs, though they have no satellite beehive dwellings.

The structures around the Amazon House area comprise two 'horned' structures with single courts and associated beehives which are still in excellent condition, and a third nearby of which little now remains. The horned approaches are, in this part of the Gleann Mor settlement, wider and more square than in other examples. One horn is longer that the other. It has been suggested that this house was the hub and centre of the culture which established them. The surrounding area, particularly on the south side, shows evidence of stone alignments or 'avenues'—small circles, monoliths and the like—all of which may have had some ceremonial significance. The whole area of Gleann Mor has never been subjected to a scientific investigation and still awaits the attention of the professional archaeologist. Systematic study might reveal what to date is often surmise, intelligent guesswork, and the conjecture posed by the evidence of a past culture in the writings of St Kilda's many visitors.

It has also been suggested that the community in Gleann Mor was coeval with that in Village Bay. There is an ancient earth-dyke extending in a wide semi-circle across the head of the glen which may well have marked the boundary between the zones of two colonies.

Boreray and Soay

Apart from the historical buildings on Hirt, there are other structures scattered throughout the St Kilda group of islands. On Boreray there is the Staller's House. Martin Martin's account of it relates:

> In the west of this Isle is Staller House, which is much larger than that of the female warrior in St Kilda, but of the same model in all respects; it is all green without, like a little hill.

MacAulay describes the house as being:

> . . . 18 feet high, and its top lies almost level with the earth, by which it is surrounded; below it is of circular form, and all its parts are contrived so that a single stone covers the top. If this stone is removed the house has a very sufficient vent. In the middle of the floor is a large hearth; round the wall is a paved seat, on which sixteen persons may conveniently sit. There are four roofed beds roofed with strong flags or strong lintels, every one of which is capable to receive four men. To

each of these beds is a separate entry, the distance between these separate openings resembling, in some degree, so many pillars.

Much of this structure is now in a ruinous state. It is said that it goes underground for 18 ft. A local tradition hints at an entrance from the house leading to a sea cave 700 ft below it. The house is traditionally that built by one Staller (stone man) who, with a large party of island adherents, rebelled against MacLeod's resident steward on the island and, taking possession of Boreray, proceeded to make it fast for himself and his followers.

On Soay island there is a building erected on a level piece of ground. There are indications that the structure was covered with turf. Tradition ascribes a religious nature to the building, it supposedly having once had an altar.

Recorded History

St Kilda's recorded history begins *c* 1380 when a charter was drawn up to enable John, Lord of the Isles, to make over some of his Hebridean islands, including St Kilda, to his son Reginald. One of Reginald's successors transferred the island group to the MacDonalds of Sleat in Skye, who subsequently gave the islands into the possession of the MacLeods of Harris, whose seat was at Dunvegan, Skye. In a MS history of the MacDonalds, written during the reign of Charles II, it is recorded that the islands had been in the possession of the MacLeods for two centuries, either through the senior branch or one of the cadet families.

In 1799 St Kilda, with Harris, was sold to Captain Alexander MacLeod for £15,000. During the next century the island changed hands twice, but always within the MacLeod family. In 1871, St Kilda was sold back again for £3,000 to Norman, twenty-second Chief of MacLeod, in whose family, the senior branch of the clan, the island group remained until Sir Reginald MacLeod sold it to the fifth Marquis of Bute in 1934.

Part of the recorded history of St Kilda involves the many shipwrecks which have occurred in the area of the island group. In 1686 a party of French and Spanish sailors were sheltered by the islanders. In 1835 a Prussian vessel foundered off St Kilda; the crew of eleven got safely ashore. They spent two weeks on the island before crossing to Skye. The expense of keeping the men for the period was 5s (25p). Likewise the crews of the *Janet Cowan* (1864) and the Austrian ship *Peti Dubrovacki* (1887) found the islanders not lacking in hospitality and desire to meet the needs of others in distress, though at times they could ill afford to do so.

LADY GRANGE

Though the history of St Kilda is meagre in the extreme, it does contain one rich episode in the abduction and subsequent imprisonment of Lady Rachel Grange on St Kilda for some seven years. Only in this episode does the island's history ever come close to the historical events of the 'outside world'.

Lady Grange was the wife of Erskine of Grange, who became a Judge of the Court of Session in Edinburgh in 1707. In 1710 he became Lord Justice-Clerk. His brother was 'Bobbing Jock', the luckless Earl of Mar who led the Rising of 1715. Lord Grange had secret Jacobite sympathies and many times held meetings with Jacobite sympathisers in his Edinburgh home. Lady Grange, on the other hand, had Hanovarian sympathies. Though they had been married for twenty years and had a family of eight children, the couple drew apart; each had peculiarities of character with which the other could not bear to live. In the end, during the course of a quarrel, Lady Grange threatened to reveal to the authorities her husband's dealings with Jacobite supporters.

Late on the night of 22 January 1732, Lady Grange, then living apart from her husband in a neighbouring house, was seized by a party of Highlanders led, it is said, by Simon Fraser, Lord Lovat, who played an important part in the Rising of 1745. She was blindfolded and carried off to the Highlands, to Castle Tiorram in Moidart. She was then taken to Skye and from there to Heisgeir Island, North Uist, where she lived for two years. In 1734, the tenant of Heisgeir Island said he could keep her in his care no longer and, with the consent of MacLeod of Dunvegan, she was taken to St Kilda. She was retained there as a prisoner under the watch of a keeper for seven years. After this period

St Kilda Jan: 20 1738.

Sir

It is agreat blessing and hapiness to a nation
when the King imployeth such a man as you are to Act
and do for him who I'm perswadid his the aw and fear
of God on him. job was a just man and a perfect and the
cause that he know not he searched out to deliver
the poor and oppressed and him that had none to help
him, a patterne for on in your office. I have the Honour
to be your Relation and I know you haive much
interest with Lord Greange if you can make Peace for
me you know the promices that is to the Peace maker
you know I'm not guilty of eny crime except that
of loveing my husband to much, he knowes very well
that he was my idol and now God his made him
a rode to Scourgeth me. * * * * * * * * * *

* *

* * * * * * * * * * * * * * * * I have given him
a much fuller account then this and he wroit it down. you may have it
I have much more to tell then this when this comes to you if you hear I'm
alive do me justice and relieve me, I beg you make all hast but if you hear I'm
dead do what you think right before God.

I am with great Respect
your Most Humble Servant
but Infortunat Cousen
Rachell Erskine

Pray you make my Compliments
to all your young Family

to the Solicitor

LETTER OF LADY GRANGE, FROM ST KILDA, 1738.

Facsimile of a letter from Lady Grange from her St Kilda prison she was taken to Assynt in western Sutherland. Finally she was taken to Skye, where she died in May 1745. She was buried in the cemetery at Trumpan in Waternish, while a mock funeral was held at Dunvegan where a coffin filled with sods was duly buried with great ceremony.

While in St Kilda, Lady Grange lived in a two-roomed hut still to be seen today. She was provided with a female servant. She described the island as a 'viled, nasty and stinking poor isle'. Over a long period she gathered together pieces of paper on which she wrote a long letter. Hiding it in a clew of thread which she had spun, and which was sent with other yarn to the market in Inverness, she managed to contact her relatives. Hearing that she was alive and not dead as they had been told, they appealed to the Government for help. A sloop of war was sent to the west coast, but failed to find the poor woman who was being continually moved about. The experiences she underwent finally drove her insane.

Her letter, which caused a great stir in Edinburgh at the time, begins with her insisting that she had committed no crime 'except that of loveing my husband to much'. The story of her abduction and subsequent adventures she describes:

> . . . upon the 22d of Jan 1732, I lodged in Margaret M'Lean house and at a little before twelve at night Mrs M'Lean being on the plot opened the door and there russed in to my room some servants of Lovats and his cousin Roderick MacLeod . . . they threw me down upon the floor in a Barbarous manner . . . they dung out some of my teeth and toere the cloth of my head and tore out some of my hair . . . they carri'd me down stairs as a corps . . .

After being carried like a lost, unwanted piece of baggage through Scotland she came to St Kilda:

> . . . Oh alas much have I suffer'd often my skin made black a blew, they took me to St Kilda. John MacLeod is called Stewart of the Island he left me in a few days no body lives in but the poor native it is a viled, nasty and stinking poor isle. I was in great miserie in the Husker (Heisker) but I am ten times worse and worse here, the Society sent a Minister here I have given him a much fuller account than this and he writ it down,

Page 107: *(above)* Gannet hunters' bothy on Sulasgeir; *(below)* the men of Ness, once settled in the bothies, prepare the long bamboo catching poles. The spring device on the end fastens round the neck of the guga which tends to retreat to the outer edge of the cliff ledges

Page 108: *(left)* Sulasgeir, gannet hunter plucking a gannet; *(right)* after gutting, the guga is salted, carefully rolled and placed on a huge stack of gugas high over the landing place to await the relief boat you may be sure I have much more to tell than this, When this coms to you if you hear I'm alive do me justes and relieve me, I beg you make all haste but if you hear I'm dead do what you think right befor God.

I am with great respect
your most humble servant
but unfortunate Cousen
Rachell Erskine

AS THEY SAW IT

The earliest known description of the Western Isles is that of Donald Monro, High Dean of the Isles. It is valuable because it is based largely on personal observation. It formed the basis of George Buchanan's account of these islands, at the beginning of his Latin *History of Scotland*. Monro's records give much detail about conditions in the Hebrides some 400 years ago. He was born about the beginning of the sixteenth century, and he was related to several of the most influential families in the Highlands and Islands of Scotland. His family also had a tradition of service in the church through whose influence he was able to aspire to high office. Donald Monro was first presented in 1526 to the vicarage of Snizort and Raasay, in Skye. Around 1547 he became an archdeacon. One of his first actions was to make himself familiar with his diocese and in 1549 he travelled through many of the islands described in his book. While his primary concern was the business of the church, his observations of the secular scene were more than useful. Monro died *c* 1576, unmarried. He was buried at Kiltearn, beside the Cromarty Firth, near the seat of his family, the Munros of Foulis. No stone marks his grave and his only monument today is the book which he never himself saw in print. Of St Kilda he says:

To the west north-west of this Ile (Uist) out of the mane Ocean seais be 60 mile of sea lyis ane Ile callit *Hirta*, mane laich sa far as is manurit of it, abundand in corn and girsing, namelie for scheip, for thai are fairer and greater scheip tair and langer taillit than thair is in ony uther Ile thairabout. The inhabitants thairof are simple creatures, scant learnit in ony

Religion: but Mccloyd of Haray his Stewart, or quhom he deputtis in sic office, sayles anes in the zeir at midsymmer with sum chaiplane to baptize bairns thair; and gif they want ane chaiplane, thai baptize thair bairns thamselfis. The said Stewart, as himself tald me, usit to tak ane mask of malt thair with ane maskein fat and mask his malt, and or the fat be readie, the commons of the town baith men, women and bairns puttis thair hand in the fat, and finding it sweit greynes eftir the sweitnes thairof, quhill neither wort nor draff are left upsuppit out thair, quhill baith men, women and bairns were deid drunken, so that thai could nocht stand on thair feet.

The said Stewartis ressaves thair maillis in maill and reistit muttonis, wild reistit foullis and selchis. This Ile is mair nor nae mile lang narrest, alsmeikle breid, quhilk is not seen of ony land or of ony schoir; But at the schoir side of it lyis three great hills, quhilk are ane pairt of Hirt, quhilk are seen far off from the forlands. In thir roch Iles are infinite fair scheippis, with ane falcon nest and wild foullis biggand. But the seais are stark and verie evill entering in ony of the saids Iles. This Ile perteinit to Mccloyd of Haray of auld.

When Martin Martin went to St Kilda in 1697 he was accompanied by Rev Mr Campbell, who had been summoned to the island to denounce a certain false prophet who had risen among its 180 inhabitants, professing to be an emissary of John the Baptist. Martin's account of the islanders is given in a tone compacted of amusement and admiration. He observed that the community was backward in some ways. They were illiterate and had many silly customs. He was full in his admiration and devotion to the St Kildans. He praised their music and their poetry, their natural courtesy and their virtue: 'The inhabitants of St Kilda are much happier than the generality of mankind, as being almost the only people in the world who feel the sweetness of true liberty.'

It was Martin's writings which attracted the attention of many others to the island, particularly writers and poets. In 1747, William Collins, a young English poet, was staying at Richmond to be close to his friend, Scotland's James Thomson, the author of *The Seasons* which was then fashionable reading. He came across Martin's account of St Kilda in Thomson's library and wrote of the autumnal bird migration.

Another friend of Thomson's, David Mallet, used St Kilda as the background to a romantic verse-tale, *Amyntor and Theodora: or The Hermit*, of 1748. This tells the story of an exiled Edinburgh Covenanter re-united to his daughter and his enemy's son by a shipwreck; there was plenty of detail extracted from Martin, and there was a prefatory note advising readers to visit the island themselves.

In 1737 an authorless poem had appeared called *Albania*. It was published in London and made mention of 'utmost Hirta's seers' among its tributes to the Isles.

James Thomson himself came under St Kilda's spell, even from a far distance and through Martin as medium:

> Or where the Northern ocean, in vast whirls
> Boils round the naked melancholy isles
> Of farthest Thule, and the Atlantic surge
> Pours in among the stormy Hebrides,
> Who can recount what transmigrations there
> Are annual made? What nations come and go?
> And how the living clouds on clouds arise?
> Infinite wings! till all the plume-dark air,
> And ride-resounding shore, are one wild cry.
> Here the plain harmless native, his small flock,
> And herd diminutive of many hues,
> Tends on the little island's verdant swell,
> The shepherd's sea-girt reign; or to the rocks
> Dire-clinging, gathers his ovarious food,
> Or sweeps the fishy shore; or treasures up
> The plumage, rising full, to form the bed
> of Luxury. ('Autumn')

In 1838, on the occasion of his visit to St Kilda, Lachlan MacLean wrote, 'I shall for the present close my journal, and that in the words of Dr MacCulloch, with some little deviation, viz:'

> If St Kilda is not the Eutopia so long sought, where will it be found? Where is the land which has neither arms, money, care, physic, politics, nor taxes? That land is St Kilda. No tax-

gatherer's bill threatens on a church door—the game-laws reach not the gannets. Safe in its own whirlwinds, and cradled in its own tempests, it heeds not the storms which shake the foundations of Europe—and acknowledging the dominion of M'Leod, cares not who sways the British sceptre.

Well may the pampered native of happy *Hirt* refuse to change his situation—his slumbers are late—his labours are light—his occupation his amusement. Government he has not—law he feels not—physic he wants not—politics he heeds not—money he sees not—of war he hears not. His state is his city—his city is his social circle—he has the liberty of his thoughts, his actions, and his kingdom and all the world are his equals. His climate is mild, and his island green, and the stranger who might corrupt him shuns its shores. If happiness is not a dweller in St Kilda, where shall it be sought?

EVACUATION

Until the years of the mid-nineteenth century, the St Kildan community seemed secure in its striking ability to maintain itself in an unsophisticated condition on a par with that found in many parts of Europe. The community enjoyed a reasonable, if modest, standard of living; and there was little difference between St Kilda and parts of the nearby Scottish mainland or western islands. The islanders were for the most part physically fit, well-clothed and satisfied. Then came the pin-pricks: the recurrent epidemics; the endemic scourge of infantile tetanus; successive failures of the harvest; the contacts which an outer world brought closer to them by visiting tourists; and the gradual realisation that, as part of an infinitely larger cash-based society, they were fast becoming anachronisms. One might say that in the end it was not insularity but isolation which killed off the St Kildan community. As if in evidence of this, one recalls the many return visits made by some of the expatriate St Kildans and their efforts to re-establish some kind of physical contact with their former homeland. One also recalls the return some years ago of the islanders of Tristan da Cunha to their island, ravaged though it was by volcanic action.

Evacuation as a solution to the islanders' increasing problems was discussed seriously in 1875, when a plan was put forward to take the entire population to Canada. Some twenty-five years before this, there had been a small evacuation which undoubtedly did the community some harm, but which it managed fitfully to survive. In 1886, a report was published in which it was said that it might be worthwhile investigating the possibility of assisting the St Kildans to emigrate, as nearly all of them wanted to leave the island.

The birth of the twentieth century saw the St Kildans no nearer to finding a solution for continued survival which would satisfy the increasing demands of sophisticated society that remote communities should either conform to a set social and economic pattern, with little room for the preservation of environmental conditions desired by their small populations—or cease to exist altogether. In August 1920, Sgt MacGillivray, writing from the Police Station at Tarbert, Harris, to his Chief Constable, said: 'I beg to report that there were 73 inhabitants on the island and there is now nobody on the island but the missionary and the natives.' This refers to the fact that damage caused by a German submarine during the 1914–18 War had been repaired and the party of workmen had now left. A year later he reported: '. . . since last year there has been one birth and one death'.

In 1928 the population was down to 37, 15 males and 22 females. Police Constable MacKay noted in a report: '. . . there is talk of some more of the natives leaving the island because the living obtained is so poor'. The following year an epidemic of wet eczema broke out, together with bad weather during which the islanders failed to gather in their crops which lay unripened in the fields waiting for the sun which never came.

The St Kildan community faced the start of 1930 with the knowledge that it was but a matter of months until the final decision was taken for the inevitable evacuation. In April 1930, the islanders' plight received the active sympathy of Mr T. B. W. Ramsay, MP for the Western Isles constituency. He wrote to the then Secretary of State for Scotland, William Adamson:

> I have written to the Highlands and Islands Distress Committee asking them to do something to help the people on the island who are in such dire straits as regards food supplies.

I hope you will do something to relieve these people in their terrible plight.

The *Scotsman* newspaper recorded that a Fleetwood trawler had brought much-needed provisions to the St Kildans who had been 'reduced to living on meal and water and salted seabirds'.

The skipper reported: 'Except one or two men who have lived all their days on the island, the rest of the inhabitants want to come to the mainland. They do not desire to face another winter of such privations.'

Now that the island was so much in the public eye, the Government was forced to step in and the then Under Secretary of State for Scotland, Mr Tom Johnston, asked for a report 'at the earliest possible moment on the possibility of bringing the inhabitants of St Kilda off the island, and settling them on the various vacant holdings which he understands exist on the Department's estates'. The department concerned was the Department of Agriculture. Mr Johnston also asked for the report to show 'an estimate of the cost'. The matter was to be regarded as peculiarly urgent since it was expected that a question about St Kilda would be raised in the House.

Subsequently, investigations produced a reply from the Department of Agriculture to Tom Johnston: 'It would appear that only one family is willing to take a holding . . . the majority wish to settle in Edinburgh or Glasgow.' This was to be a transition with a vengeance: from remote insularity, the members of a simple community were electing to become members of a vast urbanised social complex and face all the pressures with which even the conditioned indigenous city dwellers found it difficult to cope successfully.

On another tack, the department wrote to Mr Ramsay: 'The Department have seen articles in the Press referring to distress . . . they have, however, received no confirmation that there has been an acute shortage of food among the islanders.' The department had, in addition, considered the fact that the Highlands & Islands Distress Committee had decided to take no action on Mr Ramsay's representations. Mr Ramsay kept pressing the matter, however. He wrote to the island's missionary, the Rev

Dugald Munro. He received a reply which he communicated to Mr Johnston, saying that the islanders 'are uncertain as to the future . . . many hope to be assisted to leave the island this year as the unsatisfactory conditions which prevailed throughout last winter have left them very unsatisfied'. Ramsay added that he planned to visit St Kilda in an attempt to find out the true state of affairs on the island.

On 10 May 1930, the St Kildans, through the agency of the Rev Munro, sent a petition to the Scottish Secretary of State. It was signed by twenty islanders and witnessed by Munro and Williamina M. Barclay, Queen's Nurse on St Kilda.

'We the undersigned . . . hereby respectfully pray and petition Her [*sic*] Majesty's Government to assist us all to leave the island this year and to find homes and occupation for us on the mainland.' The petition had, in fact, been precipitated by the avowed intention of several men on the island to leave of their own accord and resources and take their chances on the mainland. Munro added: 'The reason why assistance is necessary is that for many years, St Kilda has not been self-supporting, and with no facilities to better our position we are therefore without the means to pay for the costs of removing ourselves and furniture elsewhere.'

The prayers, the pleadings, the slow machinery of bureaucracy turning over every nuance in the islanders' request for assistance, finally ended in the decision to evacuate. But—what would it cost? However lavish other forms of public expenditure, the comparative pence to be spent in the relief of a handful of island folk were to be laid on the table and each penny subjected to careful scrutiny before being held up in the face of the St Kildans to emphasise that the cost of their evacuation was a serious charge on Britain's mainland society. On the other hand, could the evacuation mean a long-term saving?

Early in 1930, the Department of Health for Scotland reported that public funds were providing postal, educational and nursing services at a cost of some £600 per annum. The Report observed: '. . . the decline in cultivation may be due partly to the lack of manpower and partly to indolence, the islanders having been encouraged by tourists, trawlers, &c., to expect sympathy in the practical forms of money, coal, fish &c., for the asking'. In addition to able-bodied males and their families, a fringe of dependants would also have to be removed, 'and supported either by means of parochial or similar relief'.

A health inspector visited in St Kilda in May 1930: 'The islanders are very reluctant to state the number of sheep they possess. When a question appears to suggest an enquiry into means, the number is obviously minimised and on the other hand an inquiry that suggests compensation brings out a much higher number.' He emphasised in his report the disproportionate expense of providing nursing and educational services, and, somewhat needlessly, the dangers of inbreeding, in a society which had regulated such affairs extremely well over the centuries. The island's Nurse Barclay suggested that the average earnings per household from the sale of woollen goods and eggs was about £26 per annum.

In actual fact, between 1925 and 1930, the medical and nursing service cost a total of £1,642 8s 7d. The Department of Agriculture found its St Kilda bill comparatively light: in 1926—item, bull, £40; in 1928—item, repairs to crane, £3; in 1929—item, bull, £39. Total, £82.

Another aspect of the evacuation concerned the St Kildan sheep. The problem here was catching the sheep and their subsequent transportation and sale. There were an estimated 1,500 sheep on St Kilda itself. They were so wild, however, 'that their legs might have to be tied'. A suggestion that netting might be taken out to St Kilda for impounding the stock was answered by 'we much doubt if any netting would hold in these sheep which are great jumpers'. Each sheep would bring in an estimated 15s (75p), but the removal of the sheep was not considered likely to be an economic success. The West Highland Auction Mart, approached by the Department of Agriculture to handle the St Kildan sheep, wrote back to say: '. . . would prefer to take no responsible part in it . . .' Most of the sheep were eventually rounded up by the islanders and three shepherds sent from Lewis by the government. The *Dunara Castle* took most of the livestock when she left on evacuation day.

In July 1930, the Admiralty informed Tom Johnston that

HM ships *Harebell* and *Godetia* could be made available and estimated that the cost of the service would not be above £100. The Admiralty, being literally the prime mover, and faced with a task which was they felt better carried out *in camera*, called a conference of all the parties interested, in one way or another, in the evacuation of St Kilda. The conference, according to a memorandum on the proceedings, was told that the Secretary of State was 'strongly against any official provision being made for representatives of the Press'. The delegates were told that twenty-four of the island inhabitants were going to Loch Aline, on the direct route from St Kilda to Oban.

The information caused no little alarm in Inverness-shire's County Council. The County Clerk wrote to the Department of Health to say that his council 'are a little anxious . . . that during the period of acclimatisation . . . certain of the islanders self-supporting at present, might, by reason of their transfer to the mainland, become a burden on the County'.

Tom Johnston, in an attempt to raise funds for the settlement of the St Kildans, and for help in the expenses incurred in the removal process, approached the Highland & Agriculture Society of Scotland and the Highlands & Islands Fund. The first body said that it was not proper for the money which lay in their St Kilda Fund to pay for the necessary furniture in connection with the rehousing of the islanders. They were, however, prepared to use the money for things 'over and above the bare necessities of life', such as the purchase of livestock. The Highlands & Islands Fund said that the Trustees had considered Mr Johnston's application for a £500 grant for the St Kildans but were against a direct block grant. They were willing only to consider individual cases of distress and helpfully sent off some application forms.

While official, public and semi-public bodies were treating the whole affair rather cagily, the Press, in sharp contrast, found the St Kilda story very strong meat for their columns. An official of the Health Department found time to complain in a letter to Tom Johnston:

> I am being pestered by representatives of the Press . . . I understand from the Scottish Office that it is your view that it would be unfortunate to make a public 'show' of the evacuation

and accordingly I am trying to avoid mentioning the actual date as far as possible, and am also telling the Press that the accommodation available doesn't permit . . .

But the St Kilda affair was now a public matter and was rightly considered important enough for accurate accounts of the evacuation to be recorded for posterity. One request from the Press to attend the evacuation was sent through No 10 Downing Street to the Scottish Office. The Prime Minister received the reply: 'The Admiralty are naturally hostile to the idea of publicity and Mr Johnston himself is strongly of the opinion that the utmost effort should be made to avoid the miseries of the poor people being turned into a show.' It concluded: 'The Scottish Office are endeavouring to carry out the evacuation with as little publicity as possible out of consideration for the feelings of the St Kildans themselves.'

The final estimate of the cost of the evacuation, 'no more than £500' alarmed the Treasury. 'We have been prepared from the start to deal with the situation as sympathetically as possible in the confidence that while everything necessary would be done to secure finality in resettlement of the inhabitants on the mainland you would not incur expenditure other than on a reasonable scale.' The bill for £500 was '. . . somewhat higher than we expected . . . we should wish to know beforehand if you are driven to the actual building of new houses for any of the families who have not at present any accommodation in sight'. Later the Treasury hoped 'every effort will be made to keep the amount to be borne on public funds at a minimum and to meet the requirements as far as practicable from other sources'. The cost of the evacuation was finally about £800.

The evacuation took place on 29 August 1930. Not all the islanders' possessions were removed. Much was left behind, particularly bulky furniture, chairs, pictures, looms; these and other items were left to be ravaged by wind and rain. One of the last of the St Kilda wooden-beam looms is in the possession of Mr J. G. Jeffs, of Kirkcudbright, Scotland.

The death of the St Kildan community was sensitively recorded by Surgeon Lieut-Comdr A. A. Pomfret, RN, of His Majesty's sloop *Harebell*:

At 07.00 hours all the houses were locked and the people taken on board. Shortly afterward they were looking their last at St Kilda as the *Harebell*, quickly increasing speed, left the island a blur on the horizon. Contrary to expectations they had been very cheerful throughout, though obviously very tired, but with the first actual separation came the first signs of emotion, and men, women and children wept unrestrainedly as the last farewells were said. An hour later the few remaining were landed at Oban and the evacuation of St Kilda was complete.

On the voyage from St Kilda, the thirty-six islanders were cared for with sympathy. They did not know of the ship's message to the Admiralty regarding who was to foot the bill in the matter of whether the St Kilda inhabitants were to be 'victualled on board or whether they are to make their own arrangements'. The Admiralty, in a burst of generosity, replied that the islanders should be 'victualled on board' but the cost should be charged to the Scottish Office. In the event, the St Kildans fed heartily and consumed 30 lb of bread, 10 tins of salmon, and 30 lb of M & V (meat and vegetables) ration, garnished with preserved beef and jam. The bill for this fare was 42s 6d (£2·12).

After the evacuation, there was a suggestion that the cost of the operation should be charged against the sale of the islanders' sheep, which yielded £800. This suggestion was discounted, as was the proposal to defray, in the same way, the expense of rounding up the sheep and transporting them to the mainland. In the end it was agreed to distribute the whole £800 from the sale to the islanders in proportion to their ownership. Yet it took the Press to raise the matter that the islanders had not received their money from the sale of their sheep.

Most of the able-bodied islanders were found work (a guaranteed minimum of 105 days' employment each year) with the Forestry Commission at Ardtornish in Morvern. There, the St Kildans, natives of a treeless island, found themselves tending trees. The unfamiliar environment took its toll and their subsequent history is a tragic tale. In the main, the population was an ageing one: many died soon after the transportation; others drifted back, homesick, to their deserted island during the subsequent summer seasons. During the Second World War, seven of the younger men served in the Armed Forces, patriotically fulfilling a service to society.

The full story of the evacuation is now a matter of dormant records in more than two dozen files in the Scottish Record Office, Edinburgh. They are available for inspection by anyone who wishes to unravel the threads of the complicated weave that resulted in the St Kildan Parliament's decision to cut clean away more than 1,000 years of living in Britain's most remote island group.

A former islander, Christine MacQueen, seems to have summed up the nation's failure to accept its island communities and its Scrooge-like precision over the once-for-all cost of removing the St Kildan thorn: 'The whole business from start to finish has been the work of despairing Sasunnachs.'

In 1986, St Kilda was designated as Scotland's first World Heritage site by UNESCO, joining such famous places as Stonehenge in England, the Pyramids in Egypt, the Taj Mahal in India, and the Grand Canyon in the United States. In August 1987 a ceremony was conducted in the island's tiny church, restored by volunteers. There a plaque was unveiled by the Secretary of the World Heritage Convention who spoke of St Kilda being 'a testimony to the powerful work of nature and to the tenacity but ultimate fragility of human settlement.'

The army has been on St Kilda now for thirty years, over which period the islands have been owned by the National Trust for Scotland, and leased to the Nature Conservancy Council. Despite the misgivings expressed when the army took occupation, their 30-strong garrison, keeping to their 9-acre patch, have been more than helpful to the many working parties which land on Hirt to carry out essential repairs and restoration to the buildings of the former settlement.

A recently established resident is the Great Skua, arriving in the 1970s. The St Kilda wren and mouse are still protected and evolving their special characteristics. The peaty soil supports 130 different flowering plants and almost 200 lichens. The Soay sheep numbers fluctuate between 200 and 1800; at the higher level the number is automatically reduced through overgrazing and disease.

4 NORTH RONA

ISLAND EXTRAORDINARY

NORTH RONA, for its size, is the most northerly isolated and exposed island of the British Isles ever to be regularly inhabited, probably before Scotland appeared in recorded history. Though nowadays it is often omitted from maps, it still deserves full consideration in view of the part it has played in the life of the people of the Ness district in the north of Lewis. North Rona is called 'North' to distinguish it from South Rona, an inshore island lying off Skye, and from Ronay, which lies off South Uist; it is 44 miles NNE from the Butt of Lewis and 45 miles NW from Cape Wrath. It lies in latitude 59° 7′ 30″ and longitude 5° 50′. With its sister island of Sulasgeir, North Rona forms the northern termination of the Outer Hebrides.

The island has been described as having the 'shape of a decanter with the neck towards the north'. It is some 300 acres in extent, with a maximum length, north to south, of 1 mile. The breadth at the southern end of the island is similar. The central part of Rona forms a high ridge reaching its highest point in Toa Rona, 355 ft above sea level. From this hill-ridge the ground falls away gradually to the south-west and, at its lowest part, the island is almost flush with the sea. The slopes which fall away rapidly from the ridge to the north, end in high cliffs.

The most northerly part of Rona is Fianuis, a flat peninsular rocky surface jutting out from the main land-mass of the island. At most, this part is 60 ft above sea level, varying from the cliff-edges of the west side to the gentler slopes and flat rock-bed of Leac Mhor (Big slab). The island's cliffs are tunnelled through and through with caves. One of the most impressive is the Tunnel Cave, at the head of which there is a blow-hole some 100 ft long and which appears in the surface of the ground above about the

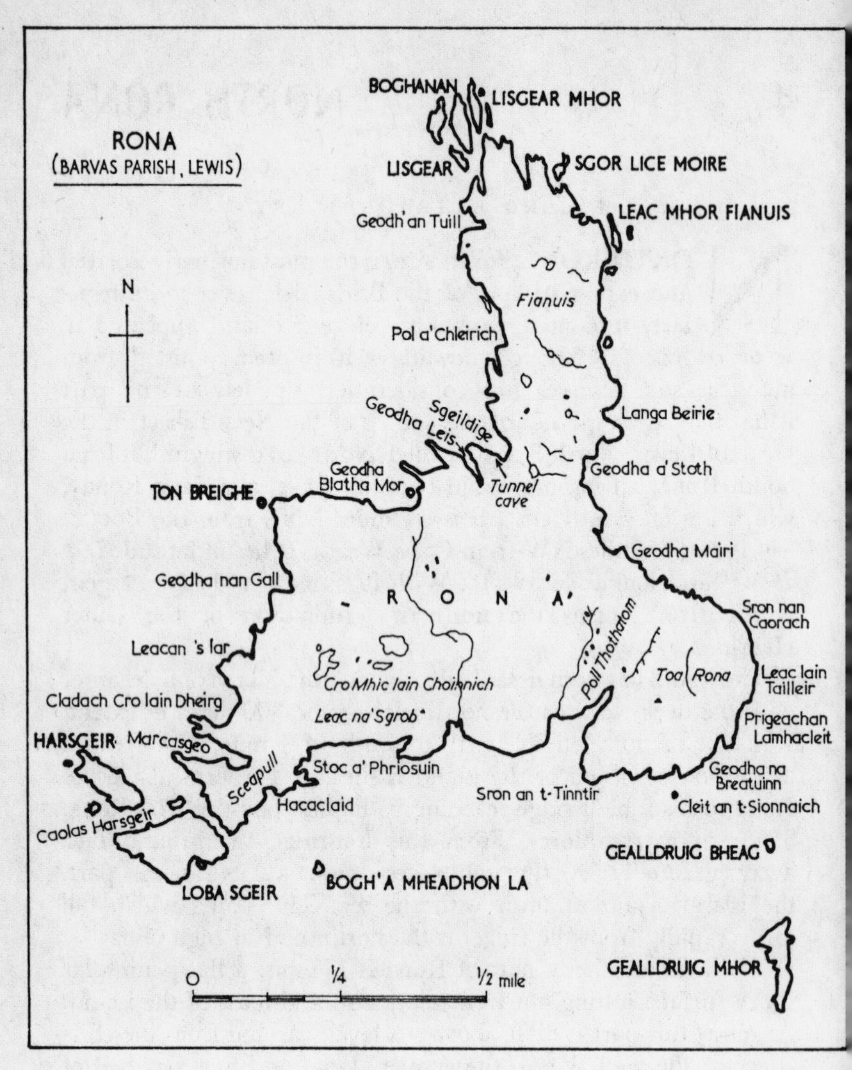

Sketch map of North Rona

middle of the neck of Fianuis. The island had no proper beach or shore. All round the island lie hidden reefs and skerries.

Occasionally one or two of these show above the water, such as the pinpricks Harsgeir and Loba Sgeir to the southwest. Farther off lies the skerry of Gealldruig Mhor. Rona is owned by a Lewisman and is used for grazing sheep.

The island is composed of Hebridean hornblende gneiss with veins of pegmatite. Quartz and felspar are also found. The rock is for the most part covered with a few inches of sandy soil held together by various kinds of organic matter and by the roots of a tenacious turf composed of Yorkshire fog, bents and fescue grasses. Some sedge is to be found to the south of the island, near the 'village'. The drier, rocky parts of Rona are covered with sea plants: sea-pink, buck's-horn plantain, scurvy grass, Scotch lovel and mayweed. Altogether some forty-one species of plants exist on the island.

As might be expected, the island is both a place of residence for an indigenous seabird population and a lodging house for migrants, who find Rona a convenient stopping-off place to rest their wings for a few days and feed up to gain the strength needed for further flight. The most common birds are kittiwakes, closely followed by fulmars. Other species include gulls, shags and Leach's petrels. These latter birds breed on only three places in the British Isles other than on North Rona: on St Kilda, the Flannans and on Sulasgeir. Recent counts by ornithologists show that North Rona is now the largest breeding station for these small midnight-blue birds which come ashore only to breed.

The name of the island is correctly derived from Ron-y, meaning Seal Island. Certainly the Atlantic grey seals breed on North Rona in greater concentration than anywhere else in the world. Their haunt is the low, flat expanse of Fianuis. The seals come ashore in the autumn to give birth to the calves.

HISTORY

The First Inhabitants

Tradition has it that the first inhabitant of the island was St Ronan, who was so exasperated with the sound of women's quarrelling voices at Ness in Lewis that he upped and went to the island which is supposed to bear his name. The story tells how Ronan prayed God for guidance on how he could effectively escape from the ceaseless babble of female tongues and devote his time exclusively to the serious thought and spiritual occupation which befitted a man of God. In a vision, St Ronan was told to go to the shore on the following morning. He did this and saw a whale which gave him the convenience of its back to make the journey to Rona.

When he landed on the island he found it inhabited by an unruly and quarrelsome mob of large ugly-looking animals, like dogs, with great long claws and red eyes which glowed like coals. In the usual manner, the saint prevailed against these beasts, with the acknowledged divine aid, and walked fearlessly towards the creatures. They, in turn, walked backwards, powerless against the superiority of the good man. They reached the edge of the cliffs and fell over, desperately clawing at the hard rock for a hold to ease their fall. They scratched in vain, however, and all plunged into the deep water. The scratch marks they left can be seen today in the form of deep channels in the face of Leac na Sgrob (Slab of the Scraping).

There were a number of saints called Ronan. One such was the Abbot of Kingarth in Bute. He, and his disciples, travelled far and wide on gospel missions, apparent proof of this being the large number of small cells bearing his name scattered throughout the Hebrides. At Eoropie, in Ness, there is Teampull Ronain, and nearby is the inevitable Ronan's Well. So this tradition may well be founded on fact. This St Ronan died in 737. Another St Ronan appears in the Irish Calendar of Saints. Little is known about this cleric except that he laboured in Scotland and was once involved in the Paschal dispute, which might be as good a reason as any for making sail for a remote island to live out the rest of one's life as a hermit. In all likelihood, the Abbot of Kingarth was the original.

Many of the saints of St Ronan's day and age were keen on travel. Like St Brendan, the Irish seafarer saint, they were attracted to lonely places to live out their lives in deep thought and meditation, as sanctuaries on earth for the Holy Spirit, far

Page 125: *(left)* The south-east cliffs of Sulasgeir, some 200 ft high; *(right)* Flannan Isles. This photograph of the West Landing was taken before the disaster on 15 December 1900

Page 126: Eilean Mor, Flannan Isles: *(above)* approach from the east; *(below)* some of the workmen employed during the construction of the lighthouse in 1899

from the secular influences which, even in those early days, were often too strong to be resisted. The fact that St Ronan was an historic person does not necessarily mean he actually visited the island and stayed there, especially as his career indicates that he had heavy administrative and other responsibilities as Abbot of Bute. More likely, as with St Columba of Iona, missionaries went abroad from these religious centres carrying the blessing and name of the current dignitary with instructions to set up cells and places of worship as visible signs that Christ was among the people of the islands. It may well be that one of these missionaries from Bute reached Lewis, travelled north through the island to Ness and heard about a resident community on Rona. Then he made his way there to become resident priest. This makes the assumption that the Norse in Lewis were amenable to Christianising influences in the eighth century. If they were not, the cell of Rona island may well date from the eleventh or twelfth century, when clerics were certainly acceptable among the emerging powerful families and clans of the Highlands.

Another tradition claims to record the first owners of Rona. This concerns the dispute between the Morisons of Ness and the people of Sutherland, on the Scottish mainland, over the ownership of the island. After a prolonged discussion, heated we may be sure, it was decided that two boats should race for the island; the first claim staked down would prove ownership for all time. The boats set off. The island's shape reared up on the horizon and as the boats skimmed over the waters the Sutherland boat seemed to draw ahead. But the Morisons had planned beforehand in the event of such a possibility. One of them shot a burning arrow onto the island and set the grassy top on fire, thus getting prior claim on the land. This tradition is probably founded on the custom of the Norsemen who, by lighting a fire at the mouth of a river, thought this act sufficient to lay claim to all the country which the river drained.

Leaving tradition aside, it can be taken as a reasonable premise that North Rona supported a population from the eighth century AD. The earlier Norsemen must have known about Rona and the other northern and western outposts of the long chain of islands comprising the Outer Hebrides. Most of these small islands have placenames of Norse and Icelandic origin. It is possible that the first settlers were itinerant Vikings who chose the island as an extremely useful base from which to operate raiding excursions on the north and west coast of Scotland.

As Rona was fertile and cultivable, and provided a diet from seabirds and their eggs, the Norsemen would hardly overlook the immense strategic possibilities of such a base. In addition, it was virtually impregnable, for to this day landing on North Rona is possible only in good weather. And even given the latter, any invaders would have to contend with rocks and the like thrown down at them from the upper landing heights. Perhaps the only disadvantage of Rona might be the fact that the bed on which Rona lies is hard rock. This makes it difficult for an anchor to hold, so that any resident ship, intermittently based on the island, would have to carry two crews, one crew remaining on the island, while the other took the ship to maraud down the nearby coasts. The ultimate take-over of the island would be with the birth of children in the settlement, for women, Norse or otherwise, were part of the baggage of the early Vikings. Thus a community would come into being.

A Fertile Island

The social history of North Rona is extremely interesting. It is that of a remote island community, relatively inaccessible to external influences, and thereby left to make progress at a pace dictated only by the necessarily limited intellect of those who made up the population. From the various accounts written of the people of Rona, certain aspects of island life emerge which indicate the slow and uneventful progress of the community to an awareness of itself and the eventual desire to fit in somehow with the scheme of things which the world outside had long since planned and implemented to meet the normal needs of the civilised human being.

In 1549, Donald Monro said of North Rona :

> Towards the north-eist or north north-eist from Leozus (Lewis) 60 miles of sea lyis ane little Ile callit Ronay, laich mane land, inhabite and manurit be simple people scant of ony Religion. This Ile is half mile lang, half mile braid : abundand of

> corn growis in it be delving, be abundante of naturall claver girs for scheip. Thair is ane certane number of ky and scheip ordanet for this Ile be thair awin auld rycht, extending to sa mony as may be sufficient upon the said girsing; and the countrie is sa fertile of girsing, that the superexcrescens of the said ky and scheip baith feidis thame in flesche and als payis thair dewties with the same for the maist pairt.
>
> Within this Ile thair is sic fair quhyte beir meill maid like flowir, and quhan thay slay thair scheip (they slay them) belly flauchts and stuffs the said skynnis fresche of the beir meill. They send thair dewtie aftirwart to Mccloyd of Leozus, with certane reistit muttonnis. and mony reistit wild fowls. Within this Ile thair is ane chapell callit St Ronans chapell, into the quhilk chapell (as the ancients of that cuntrie alledgis) they use to leave ane spaid and ane schoole quhan one deid, and upon the morn findis the place of the grave taiknit with ane spaid (as thai alledge). In this Ile they use to tak mony quhaillis and utheris great fisches.

Even in those days when many another island and Scottish-mainland community was considered remote, the community on North Rona, being so small compared with, for instance, that on St Kilda, must have seemed on the very edge of the world, if not just beyond it. Yet the island and its community was significant, for it demonstrated that Man could inhabit such a place and, with his simplest requirements satisfied, form a vigorous self-dependent and self-supporting community.

As Monro says, the island could well support its community, any supplementary dietary needs were provided by the seals and the seabirds. Considering the extremely barren nature of its sister isle Sulasgeir, North Rona was surprisingly fertile. The produce of the island was sufficient not only to meet all domestic requirements but to leave a surplus to pay for the Rona rent or tribute to MacLeod of Lewis, chief of that clan at Stornoway, or for trading. Of course, such a community was ever at the mercy of marauders, mainly seamen from passing ships who let their desire for fresh meat so overpower them that they raided the island's larder. This, in fact, happened on at least one occasion in the island's recorded history.

Though it lacked some essentials (for instance, peat for fuel) the island supported or produced sheep, cows, a bull for breeding, oats, milk products, corn, barley meal, wild-fowl feathers, potatoes, mutton, seabird carcases, and seal skins. Monro mentions 'whales and other great fishes', though this might well be an assumption, for this type of fishing activity implies the possession of a boat able to carry a crew of at least four. As there is no beach on Rona it is difficult to see how or where such a craft could be drawn up to safety above high-water mark. A small light canoe-type craft or kyak might have been available for light fishing, but certainly it would have been unsuitable for whaling. Accounts do not mention that fishing was an occupation of significance, except to indicate the existence of fishing rights around the island. As dried fish, fish-oil and the like do not figure in the island's list of produce, fishing was apparently pursued for domestic purposes only: a change of diet, a source of manure, oil for lamps, or dried fish to be stored and used for food during the winter months.

Sir George MacKenzie's account, quoted more fully later in the chapter, and which is probably derived from hearsay, tells us that the community was organised as 'a kind of commonwealth'. However, the principle of sharing goods and of communal existence seemed to extend only to the equalising of the numbers of each family. There were five families, each with six persons, making thirty the optimum maximum total at any one time. This number seemed to be critical. If it were exceeded, the surplus persons had to be removed to Lewis. There seems to be no indication who these persons were, whether young, teenage, old, or male or female. The population of Rona was often less than thirty.

While still a 'commonwealth', there was a definite delineation of property in the allotment of parts of the shores and perhaps inshore sea areas for fishing. Martin tells us that none of the islanders would 'by any means allow his neighbour to fish within his property'.

Tragedy

The little community which Monro had found so pleasantly prosperous, met tragedy in the latter part of the seventeenth century. Martin's account of Rona is given later in this chapter. In it he tells that, about 1680, a swarm of rats, 'but none knows how', came to Rona and soon ate up all the corn on the island. These rats possibly came from a large amount of washed-up wreckage. They swarmed over the island consuming valuable supplies and starved the population. Only a few months later, this disaster was followed by a raid on the island by seamen from a passing ship who deprived the islanders of their one and only bull. 'These misfortunes and the want of supply from Lewis for the space of a year occasioned the death of all that ancient race of people'.

In such a way did the keen knife-edge, on which the Ronans lived, move to sever a thread of continuous occupation which had probably lasted for at least 1,000 years.

A Brief Colonisation

There seems to have been a short-lived colonisation of the island soon after the total loss of the original population. It too ended disastrously *c* 1695 when most of the men of the community seem to have been lost in a tragic disaster, after which the women were brought back to Lewis. This mass loss of males certainly implies a boating disaster. Possibly, after the experience of the rats and the subsequent raiding by seamen who stole the island's only bull, an attempt was made to establish a less tenuous and intermittent island contact with Lewis by keeping a boat on the island. It may have been drawn up, but with difficulty, on the storm beach to the north of the island. After this disaster, it was merely a matter of implanting a shepherd family to look after the sheep belonging to the Ness tacksman. From this time onwards, the resident population was purely functional and incidental, with no social overtones to continue the almost certain millenium of community occupation on the island. One wonders how long the community would have survived had the seventeenth-century disaster not occurred. It took the St Kildan community until the 30s of the twentieth century to finally concede defeat against overwhelming odds imposed by contemporaneous factors.

One-Family Island

By 1797, the *Old Statistical Account of Scotland* recorded only one family living on Rona, instead of the five (about thirty people) who once lived there. Walker, who published an economic history of the Hebrides in 1808, gave the population of the island as 9. The family was that of the person employed by the tacksman, the renter of the island, to look after the stock grazing. The tacksman was a native of Ness who paid £4 sterling per annum for the use of Rona. Each season he sent out a large boat to bring back corn, butter, cheese, a few sheep, and sometimes a cow. There were in addition the inevitable wild fowl and feathers.

'It is the total seclusion of Rona from all the concerns of the world which confers on it that intense character of solitude with which it seemed to impress us all . . . Rona is forgotten, unknown; for ever fixed, immovable in the dreary and waste ocean'. So wrote Dr John MacCulloch after his visits between 1811 and 1821. In his time there were about 6 or 7 acres under cultivation producing barley, oats and potatoes. 8 bolls of barley and 8 stones of gannets' feathers were sent to the Ness tacksman each year. The island grazed some 50 sheep.

The shepherd on Rona was called MacCagie. His family consisted of his wife, two boys, an infant and an old, deaf mother. There was no boat. The oil derived from coal-fish served for light. The one and only fire on the island was kept burning day and night, for should it go out it could never be re-kindled again. MacCagie had neither matches, flint nor steel to strike a spark. The family lived in very primitive conditions, in the earth-houses on the island. The children were ill-clad but healthy and well-fed. MacCagie's only worry seemed to have been his desire to have his child christened in Lewis.

The last family to live on Rona was that of Donald MacLeod, self-styled 'King of Rona', of whom it was said that he was the second monarch ruling in the British Isles at the time of his evacuation in 1844, the seventh year of Queen Victoria's reign. Since that time Rona has not had continuous habitation. Annually, men from Lewis went to the island to shear the sheep and replace a few of the stock. Sir James Matheson, who bought the island of Lewis in 1844 for £190,000, offered North Rona to the Government in 1850 for use as a penal settlement. The offer was refused.

Two Exiles on Rona

After 1844 Rona lay deserted, slowly reverting to its natural wild state. But in May 1884, the island became a haven for two men from Ness. Harvie-Brown investigated the circumstances of this migration and has left us with his findings, including his account of the subsequent tragic death of the new inhabitants of Rona:

> The names of the two men who went from Lewis to Roney were Murdoch MacKay and Malcolm MacDonald, two good representatives of the Danish and Celtic types. Having objections to the appointment of a layman as preacher to the church at Ness, and being grieved at some feeling shown them in consequence of the action which they took along with a few others of the congregation, they were desirous of making some atonement for their opposition, and resolved to leave the place.
>
> Accordingly, on the morning of Monday, 20th May, 1884, they sailed for the island of North Roney, where they landed that night. Ostensibly their reason for going there was to take care of the sheep on the island, but in reality it was to atone for their action against the minister that they went into exile. Twice did boats go out to North Roney—in the following August and September—and the friends endeavoured to get the two men to return to their families and friends, but in vain.
>
> The men were then in good health, and apparently enjoyed their island home, and employed themselves in building sheep fanks, fishing, and killing seals. It was only, however, on the 22nd April, 1885, after two previous unsuccessful attempts, that they (friends from Ness) effected a landing. No one met them. At the door of the little half-underground house occupied by the two men the boatmen found the body of Malcolm MacDonald in a sitting position beside an improvised fireplace, as if he had fallen asleep. On the floor of the house, beside the fireplace, lay the body of Murdoch MacKay. His tartan plaid was placed neatly and carefully over and under him, showing that the deft hands and the warm heart of Malcolm MacDonald had performed the last sad office to the body of his dead friend. The bodies were wrapped in canvas wrappings, and buried side by side in the primitive and beautifully situated burial-place adjoining.
>
> It was feared that the poor men might have met with foul

play, and the matter having been brought up in Parliament, the Crown authorities ordered an investigation. Accordingly, the procurator-fiscal, Stornoway, and two medical men, proceeded to Roney in the fishing cutter 'Vigilant'. The bodies of the two men were exhumed, and a post-mortem examination made.

There was no appearance of foul play; it was ascertained that Murdoch MacKay died of acute inflammation of the right lung and left kidney, and that Malcolm MacDonald died from cold, exposure and exhaustion. The opinion among the friends is that Malcolm MacDonald assiduously attended his friend day and night till he died, by which time he himself became so weak that he could not bury the body, and being unable to remain in the hut had sat down by the improvised fire and died. There was a small pot on the little fireplace at the door, indicating that Malcolm MacDonald meant to prepare for himself some food, which, however, he was never destined to eat. The medical examiners found nothing in his stomach but a few grains of meal and a little brown liquid—probably tea. An abundance of unconsumed food was found in the hut.

On this occasion the son of Malcolm MacDonald took two coffins with him to Roney, and the two friends were re-interred again side by side as before. Mr John Ross, jun., joint-fiscal, Stornoway, Dr Roderick Ross, Barvas, and Dr Finlay MacKenzie, Stornoway, Mr Gordon, Inspector of Police, Captain MacDonald of the 'Vigilant', together with some of the officers and several of the crew; MacDonald, son of Malcolm MacDonald, and one or two other relatives of the deceased men, attended the re-interment, which all present felt to have been of a touching nature.

The men would seem to have spent their time in prayer and meditation, and in reading the Gaelic Scriptures, in which they were well versed. Neither of them could write, but they kept a record of their time—of the days, weeks and the months—in a very ingenious manner. This was accomplished by means of a bar of red pine wood, evenly and accurately dressed, 2 feet long and 1⅛ inch in the side. A notch is neatly cut in the corner of the bar for each day of the week, and then a deeper notch for Sunday, while for the end of the month a cut is made from side to side of the bar. The plan is simple, clever and intelligible. The markings begin on Friday, the 21st June 1884,

> and cease on Tuesday, the 17th February, 1885. Towards the end the notches are less neatly and accurately made, indicating very clearly that the deft fingers which fashioned the rest were becoming weak and powerless to cut into the hard pine wood. These notches are no less touching than instructive, and speak to the eye and to the heart and the imagination with a pathos all their own. Through a hole in the end of the calendar is a looped cord by which to suspend the stick . . .

Harvie-Brown, referring to his own visit to North Rona continues:

> The habit of sheep-stealing is still carried on by passing ships or fishermen. In the summer of this year (1885) both sheep and the oil barrels and the plenishings of the house belong to the dead men, consisting of sugar, tea, butter, soap, a grinding-stone, etc., were stolen by some Grimsby fishermen, who have since been apprehended. These articles were all upon the island at the time of our visit in June, and there seemed to be considerable honourable feeling even amongst the proprietors against touching the dead men's effects . . .

Later, the friends of the dead men returned to Rona to erect a memorial stone among the cruder efforts of past Rona generations. The stone reads:

'SACRED TO THE MEMORY OF MALCOLM M'C DONALD NESS WHO DIED AT RONA FEB 18 1885 AGED 67 ALSO M M'C KAY WHO DIED AT RONA SAME TIME Blessed are the dead who die in the Lord.'

AS THEY SAW IT

With most now-deserted islands, their history is to be found largely in the accounts written and left by their many visitors through the centuries. North Rona is no exception. The quality of the accounts vary. Some, like MacCulloch's, give some useful facts and glimpses of life but deal at much greater length with very general impressions. Others made more purposeful visits to record the natural life on the island; while others, perhaps even more specialised, confined themselves to a close study of rocks and minerals.

The earliest account is that of Dean Monro, given already in this chapter. It is short, and concentrates on the produce of the island and the religious character of the islanders. His island-going was functional, mainly to discover the fertility and worth of church lands, which perhaps explains his interest in this aspect to the general exclusion of others. We may take the dean's remark that the folk were 'scant of onie religion' to mean that they did not possess one of the more acceptable forms of worship, and were in fact performing religious ceremonies which resembled the contemporary practice and which also contained elements not appropriate to Christianity.

About a century and a half after Dean Monro came Martin Martin, 'Gent' from Skye. He did not visit the island himself but he nevertheless recorded a great deal about the inhabitants of North Rona. While in Lewis, he was fortunate in meeting up with the Rev Daniel Morison, Minister of Barvas Parish which contained Rona, who had recently returned from a trip there, and who was still full to the brim with impressions and anecdotes.

Perhaps it was more than fortunate that the minister's account was taken down by Martin, for he does not seem to have left any other record of his visit. As it is, Morison's account, as noted down by Martin, is perhaps the most useful we have. For, though the economic aspects of Rona are not dealt with as fully as we might wish, it is sufficiently detailed to tell us of the way of life, philosophy, community organisation, social relationships and the economic condition of the island's inhabitants. It also tells of a remote people whose mental evolution had proceeded undisturbed by alien thought or action, making its own gradual progress.

> The island Rona is reckoned about 20 leagues from the north-east point of Ness in Lewis, and is counted but a mile in length, and about half a mile in breadth: it hath a hill in the west part, and is only visible from the Lewis in a fair summers-day. I had an account of this island, and the custom of it, from several natives of Lewis, who had been to the place; but more particularly from Mr Daniel Morison, minister of Barvas, after his return from Rona island, which then belonged to him as part of his glebe. Upon my landing (says he) the natives received me very affectionately, and addressed me with their usual

salutation to a stranger: "God save you pilgrim, you are heartily welcome here; for we have had repeated apparitions of your person among us (after the manner of second sight) and we heartily congratulate your arrival in this our remote country".

One of the natives would needs express his high esteem for my person by making a turn round me sun-ways, and at the same time blessing me, and wishing me all happiness; but I bid him let alone that piece of homage, telling him I was sensible to his good meaning towards me; but this poor man was not little disappointed, as were also his neighbours; for they doubted not that this ancient ceremony would have been very acceptable to me: and one of them told me, that this was a thing due to my character from them, as to their chief and patron, and they could not, nor would not, fail to perform it.

They conducted me to the little village where they dwell, and in the way thither there were three enclosures; and as I entered each of these, the inhabitants severally saluted me, taking me by the hand, and saying, "Traveller, you are welcome here." They went along with me to the house that they had assigned for my lodging; where there was a bundle of straw laid on the floor, for a seat for me to sit on. After a little time was spent in general discourse, the inhabitants retired to their respective dwelling houses; and in this interval they killed each man a sheep, being in all five, answerable to the number of their families. The skins of the sheep were entire, and flayed off so from the neck to the tail, that they were in form like a sack. These skinnes, being flayed off after this manner, were by the inhabitants instantly filled with barley-meal; and this they gave me by way of a present: one of their number acted as speaker for the rest, saying, "Traveller, we are very sensible of the favour you have done us in coming so far with a design to instruct us in our way to happiness, and at the same time to venture yourself on the great ocean; pray be pleased to accept this small present, which we humbly offer as an expression of our sincere love to you".

This I accepted, though in a very course address; but it was given with such an air of hospitality and goodwill, as deserved thanks. They presented my man also with some pecks of meal, as being likewise a traveller: the boat's-crew having been in

Rona before were not reckoned strangers, and therefore there was no present given them, but their daily maintenance.

There is a chapel here dedicated to St Ronan, fenced with a stone-wall round it; and they take care to keep it neat and clean, and sweep it every day. There is an altar in it, on which there lies a big plank of wood about 10 feet in length; every foot has a hole in it, and in every hole a stone, to which the natives ascribe several virtues: one of them is singular, as they say, for promoting speedy delivery to a woman in travail. They repeat the Lord's Prayer, Creed, and Ten Commandments in the chapel every Sunday morning. They have cows, sheep, barley and oats, and live a harmless life, being perfectly ignorant of most of those vices that abound in the world. They know nothing of money or gold, having no occasion for either; they neither sell nor buy, but only barter for such little things as they want; they covet no wealth, being fully content and satisfied with food and raiment; though at the same time they are very precise in the matter of property among themselves; for none of them will by any means allow his neighbour to fish within his property; and every one must exactly observe not to make any encroachment on his neighbour. They have an agreeable and hospitable temper for all strangers; they concern not themselves about the rest of mankind, except the inhabitants in the north part of Lewis. The take their surname from the colour of the sky, rainbow and clouds. There are only five families in this small island, and every tenant has his dwelling-house, a barn, a house where their best effects are preserved, a house for their cattle, and a porch on each side of the door to keep off the rain or snow. Their houses are built with stone and thatched with straw, which is kept down with ropes of the same, poised with stones. They wear the same habit with those in Lewis, and speak only Irish (Gaelic). When any of them comes to Lewis, which is seldom, they are astonished to see so many people. They much admire greyhounds, and are mightily pleased at the sight of horses; and one of them, observing a horse to neigh, asked if that horse laughed at him. A boy from Rona perceiving a colt running towards him, was so much frightened at it, that he jumped into a bush of nettles, where his whole skin became full of blisters.

Another of the natives of Rona having had the opportunity of travelling as far as Coul, in the Shire of Ross, which is the seat of Sir Alexander MacKenzie, everything he saw was surprising to him; and when he heard the noise of those who walked in the rooms above him, he presently fell to the ground, thinking thereby to save his life, for he supposed that the house was coming down over his head.

When Mr Morison the minister was in Rona, two of the natives courted a maid with intention to marry her; and being married to one of them afterwards, the other was not a little disappointed, because there was no other match for him in this island. The wind blowing fair, Mr Morison sailed directly for Lewis; but after three hours sailing was forced back to Rona by a contrary wind: and at his landing the poor man that had lost his sweetheart was overjoyed, and expressed himself in these words, "I bless God and Ronan that you are returned again, for I hope you will now make me happy, and give me a right to enjoy the woman every other year by turns, so that both may have issue by her". Mr Morison could not refrain from smiling at this unexpected request, chid the man for his unreasonable demand, and desired him to have patience for a year longer, and he would send him a wife from Lewis; but this did not ease the poor man who was tormented with the thought of dying without issue.

Another who wanted a wife, and having got a shilling from a seaman that happened to land there, went and gave this shilling to Mr Morison, to purchase him a wife in Lewis, and send her to him, for he was told that this piece of money was a thing of extraordinary value; and his desire was gratified the ensuing year.

About 14 years ago a swarm of rats, but none knows how, came into Rona, and in a short time, ate up all the corn in the island. In a few months after, some seamen landed there, who robbed the poor people of their bull. These misfortunes and the want of supply from Lewis for the space of a year, occasioned the death of all that ancient race of people. The steward of St Kilda being by a storm driven there told me that he found a woman with her child on her breast, both lying dead at the side of a rock. Some years after, the minister (to whom the island belongeth) sent a new colony to the island with suitable supplies. The following year a boat was sent to them with some more supplies, and orders to receive the rents; but the boat being lost as it is supposed, I can give no further account of this late plantation. The inhabitants of this little island say that the cuckoo is never seen or heard, but after the death of the Earl of Seaforth, or the minister.

It is a pity that the accounts of the conversation between Morison and the island folk were rendered into an acceptable form of language. The island language was, of course, Gaelic. So it would have been more than interesting had the minister caused Martin Martin to set down the literal account of his talks, to compare whether Gaelic had developed in Rona at the same pace as among the larger Gaelic-speaking communities. The social and economic intercourse between North Rona and Ness, in Lewis, might well have progressed the Rona Gaelic to the state where it equalled contemporary use. But, as the intercourse was intermittent and the contacts of short duration, the Rona Gaelic might have been shown to be lacking in extent of vocabulary and to be full of archaic forms of words and expressions.

The Rev Morison was displeased at the sun-ways turns of the Ronans round him as part of a blessing of welcome and says that it was an ancient ceremony. To go 'with the sun' was, in fact, common practice throughout the Highlands. Going against the sun, or widdershins, could invite the attentions of evil agencies in a number of forms, particularly faeries. There is no mention of the folklore of Rona, which is a pity, for any observations made on the superstitions or beliefs of the island folk would have been valuable as a basis for assessing the intellectual growth of the community.

Dr John MacCulloch was an expert geologist who spent the decade between 1811 and 1821 sailing among the Hebrides. After a number of unsuccessful attempts at landing on Rona he eventually succeeded. But the island itself was not the only obstacle to his ambition to get onto it and onto some of the other islands on his list: '. . . the map-makers had forgotten them, and the manufacturers of longitudes and lattitudes had tabulated them, each according to his own fancy or belief'. He said of Rona:

The first objects we saw as we reached the surface of the cliff, were a man and a boy, who, with a dog, were busily employed in collecting and driving away a small flock of sheep. No houses were visible; but, a little farther off, we perceived two women, each loaded with a large bundle, who seemed to have arisen out of the ground, and were running with all speed towards the northern side of the island. It was plain that they had taken us for pirates or Americans.

MacCulloch visited the shepherd (MacCagie) and his family:

. . . I had not observed that our conference (with MacCagie) was held on the top of a house; roof it could not be called. The whole spot seemed to consist of an accumulation of turf stacks, and, on the lowest of these, we thought ourselves stationed. It was the house itself . . . We could not perceive the entrance till it was pointed out. This was an irregular hole, about four feet high, surrounded by turf; and, on entering it, with some precaution, we found a long tortuous passage, somewhat resembling the gallery of a mine, but without a door, which conducted us into the penetralia of this cavern.

From the rafters hung festoons of dried fish; but scarcely an article of furniture was to be seen, and there was no light but that which came through the smoke-hole. There was a sort of platform, or dais, on which the fire was raised, where the old woman and her charge sat; and one or two niches, excavated laterally in the ground, and laid with ashes, seemed to be the only bed places. Why these were not furnished with straw, I know not; and, of blankets, the provision was as scanty as that of the clothes. Possibly, ashes may make a better and softer bed than straw; but it is far more likely that Kenneth MacCagie and his family could not be fashed to make themselves more comfortable. . . . Every thing appeared wretched enough; a climate where winter never dies; a smoky subterranean cavern; rain and storm; a deaf octogenarian mother; the wife and children half naked; and, to add to all this, solitude, and a prison from which there was no escape. Yet they were well fed, seemed contented, and little concerned with what the rest of the world was doing.

The short account of Rona by Sir George MacKenzie is interesting because it illustrates just how finely balanced was the

North Rona economy. Even one person too many on the island could be responsible for the death of the community, or for its continued existence, on a greatly attenuated level, until the annual relief ship came from Lewis.

> Rona had for many generations been inhabited by five families, which seldom exceed thirty souls in all; they had a kind of commonwealth among them, in so far if any of them have more children than another, he that had fewer took from the other what his number equalled, and the excresence of above thirty souls was taken with the summer boat to the Lewis to the Earl of Seaforth, their master, to whom they paid yearly some quantity of meal stitched up in sheep's skins, and feather of sea fowls.
>
> They have no fuel for fire upon the island; but by the special providence of God, the sea yearly casts in so much timber as serves them : their sheep there have wool, but of a bluish colour. There is a chapel in the midst of the isle, where they meet twice or thrice a day. One of the families is hereditary beddal (beadle), and the master of that stands at the altar and prayeth, the rest kneel upon their knees and join with him. The religion is the Romish religion : there is always one who is the chief, and commands the rest, and they are so well satisfied with their condition that they exceedingly bewail the condition of those, as supernumerary, they must send out of the island.

At much later dates, after the desertion of the island, the accounts of Rona become quite numerous. However, they are the descriptions of visiting naturalists and are interesting for details of natural life on the island and also for the picture of a once-inhabited island slowly reverting to a wild state.

When Harvie-Brown landed on North Rona it was June 1887 :

> Thrift filled the air with delicious fragrance, faint but sweet. Huge caverns, geos, gloups, and rock-arches, stacks, and detached masses of rock, abound, and at once attract attention; and the booming of unbroken Atlantic waves, and giant rollers lashing deep into their recesses, and filling often to the roof some of the great arches, proved a very fascinating scene to me.

Page 143: *(above)* View of the western cliffs of the Flannan Isles from near the West Landing showing the channel between Eilean Mor and Eilean Tighe, with puffins—sea parrots—in the foreground; *(below)* taking blackface sheep off Eilean Mor, Flannan Isles

Page 144: *(above)* Low water at Port Roy, Ceann Ear, Monach Isles; the mountains of South Uist may be seen dimly on the horizon;

(centre) on the left the schoolhouse on Ceann Ear, and on the right the last cottage on the Monach Isles to be inhabited;

(below) ferrying cattle from Heisgeir Island, North Uist

The Duchess of Bedford landed on Rona in 1907 and 1910. Her main attention was drawn to the memorial stone which had been erected to the two men who died in 1885 :

> The horrible modern tombstone erected to the memory of the last two inhabitants who died there in 1887 (*sic*), and placed in the little chapel yard amongst the old locally carved stone crosses, had been re-whitewashed. If ever I commit sacrilege it will be here.

The Duchess, who held an 'A' license and who disappeared in 1937 on a flight over the North Sea, had other things to say of the island :

> . . . by no stretch of the imagination could I have detected its (the thrift) fragrance amidst the all-pervading stench of the nesting-places of hundreds of Fulmars, Great and Lesser Black-backed Gulls and Herring Gulls.

Malcolm Stewart published his book *Ronay* in 1933, and opened up a flood of interest in the island. He visited North Rona in 1930 and 1932 :

> First impressions are always most important, for they are present in the mind when one looks back on places visited in the past. No one could ever fail to experience immense pleasure on first landing on North Rona. A narrow strip of land, on the north end covered with green vegetation and surrounded on three sides by the ever-present Atlantic. The natural stillness and the solitude of the place are broken by the cries of sea fowl, and the beat of the waves. You may be alone here on North Rona, but for all that the island is teeming with other animal life. Two hundred sheep, and milliards of gulls, not to mention the seals that are ever inhabitants of North Rona. Well they know the beauties of the place, but few let out their secret to the poor human.
>
> Ruins of villages deserted for many a year usually induce a feeling of despondency and regret, not to mention solitude, but here, however, though one stands and ponders upon the men who lived here before, no one has such thoughts of sadness. So old are the buildings and so unique their construction, that now they are entirely overgrown with turf, and only a few feet above the surface are almost indistinguishable from the surrounding ground.

HEARTH AND ALTAR

Tradition has it that after St Ronan had cleared North Rona of wild and hairy beasts, he built himself a rude stone shelter. But though he had rid the island of the physical manifestations of evil, the spirit of the Devil was still abroad and was the source of a great wind which blew on Rona and bore its full force on the saint's simple structure. But Ronan leaned against the inside wall and prevented the Devil from completing his intention of ridding Rona of such a holy man. This tradition indicates that from those earliest times the island's exposure to high winds created a problem in the design of the buildings which were to serve as dwelling houses for the island's community. To obtain adequate protection and to present as little wind-catching surface as possible, the houses were constructed as roofed dug-outs.

In many ways, the Rona houses resembled the beehive houses which are found in various parts of Lewis, ie partly underground and roofed over with either turf or large flat stones. The walls on Rona were built up from dry stones. The houses were completely without windows and chimneys. Shelving was usually built into the thicknesses of the walls; it was easy enough to do this with thin flat stones. The shelves were useful for bowls of milk and utensils to be stood out of the way. The doorway was a low corridor and one had to stoop and crawl in order to gain entrance to the living quarters. Sometimes two flimsy wicker frames served as doors to keep out the cold air.

The 'village' on Rona is now in ruins. The roofs of each cluster of dwellings have fallen in and the grassy turf has covered much of the scars left by a thousand years of occupation by man. Each cluster of dwellings contains low passages, such as that through which Dr MacCulloch made his way. Both barn and byre were part of the house, as they were in the 'black houses' of Lewis. The plan of the Rona houses is round rather than the Lewis rectangular; wind-baffling passages are distinctive.

T. S. Muir, who visited Rona in 1857, toured the island and made many observations. On his return to Lewis he met up with Iain MacKay, who had lived on Rona and whose memory of life on the island went back to the turn of the century. In some ways,

Muir and MacKay were what Martin Martin and Daniel Morison had been in the previous century: the visitor recording the other's experience of the island. MacKay asked Muir whether he had seen the Rona houses.

> Yes; and some with low stone-covered passages, partly sunk into the ground, leading crookedly into them: these passages were not in the least broken down—having been very strongly built—but the houses themselves were roofless, and empty of everything; only there was a quern, or the like, still lying about here and there.

Artist's impression of the church ruins on North Rona

St Ronan's Chapel

The structure which has the greatest interest and, perhaps, the greatest relevance to the island, is the chapel or cell of St Ronan. Unlike the secular structures, the chapel is mainly proud of the land, though still conforming to the pit-house design. It is a two-chambered building, consisting of a chancel and a nave. Iain MacKay also told T. S. Muir of the manner in which the cell was kept in good repair:

> We laid turf also on the top of the chapel, and put lime made from shells in among the stones, to keep them together; for we thought a great deal of the teampull, and would not have liked it to fall down . . . I mind we were often on the top of it putting on turfs; for the wind was always blowing them off in the winter time, so that we had every now and then to be putting them on again.

When Dr Frank Fraser Darling visited North Rona in 1939 to spend some time on the island, he passed some of the days by doing some excavation work on the chapel. It was his work which restored the chapel to its original state. In his book *Island Years* he describes his activity:

> Tradition has it that St Ronan built the existing cell on Rona, and as this building is in many ways typical of the cells built by ascetic hermits of the early Celtic Church in other parts of Scotland, there is no reason yet for disbelieving the traditional origin of a building which is unlike any other on Rona.
>
> Muir, a Scottish ecclesiological antiquary, who visited Rona in 1857 and 1860, made careful measurements of the cell and described the place as he found it. His sketches indicate a very long entrance, and a paving to the cell is implied. He also wrote of entering the cell on elbows and knees; it was the unlikelihood of this being the original mode of ingress that decided me to dig.
>
> The east and west walls are almost perpendicular, but the longer north and south walls slope inwards rapidly, and at a height of over eleven feet are bridged by rectangular slabs of gneiss to finish the roof. The length and breadth of the cell at floor level are 11 feet 6 inches and 8 feet. This building is in drystone, very beautifully done, and the technique is the same as that of the black houses still inhabited in Lewis. The inside edges of the flattish stones are set a little higher than those reaching to the outside, so that all water draining on to the top of such a wall must drain outwards and the inside surface remains dry and free from condensation. The beehive shielings are built on the same principle and the courses reach inwards from near the foot of the wall. These buildings are in direct descent from the culture of the Megalithic age. St Ronan's cell is the best example of this type of construction I know, and into the south wall, near the east end, he built a neat aumbry a foot

square. There is a small window 19 inches by 8 inches running through the thickness of the west wall above the door. Whether there was a similar window in the east end is not known, because the upper part of the wall there has fallen in. Earth and stones were banked high round the north, east and south walls so that the building was practically underground. The outside of the west wall became the east inside wall of a chapel which was built some time after Ronan's cell; Muir estimated about two centuries later. This building, also in drystone but of poorer workmanship, is 14 feet 8 inches long by 8 feet 3 inches, and forms in effect a nave to the cell as chancel. But it is doubtful whether the two buildings were used conjointly in this way.

The roof and much of the walls of the chapel have disappeared, and when I first went to Rona the south wall was just a heap of stone fallen outwards. I had with me a copy of Harvie-Brown's book aforementioned, in which there is what is probably the first photograph of the chapel ever taken. That was in 1885. The south wall was erect then, and from the photograph I could see very well the height of the doorway in the south wall and a curious bulge in the eastern half of that wall. I began nervously to make a clearance of the fallen stones and to find the foundations; I did not wish to take down much in an effort to rebuild, for there was no knowing where I should be able to stop. However, once the foundation was clear, even showing that increased thickness east of the doorway, I went ahead with confidence. The south wall is now back in the state it was in 1885, and I do not think it will be easy to tell where I began my work.

I now turned my attention to the inside of the chapel, which had been occupied by fulmar petrels in the summer and was half full of fallen stone and earth. This very low doorway into the cell was intriguing, and it was there I struck first with spade and pick. It was not long, as I cleared my way north and south of the opening, before I struck two blocks of masonry; they were piers 3 feet high and 2 feet 3 inches square, one each side of the entrance, and they had at some time been faced with lime mortar. When I reached the foot of these piers, which I take to be the altar supports of the chapel, I found a rough paving running into the doorway of the cell. Here was no necessity for elbows and knees; the doorway and its original paving and a tiny step was 4 feet 4 inches high and 20 inches broad. The vertical section of soil and floor made by my digging revealed a thick bed of shell sand laid on the paving over the floor of the chapel. I found charred bones of sea birds and seals in this layer. A hard floor of rammed clay lay above the shell sand, and I was able to clear all the inside of the chapel to the level of the clay. As the east end and the entrance to the cell showed workings below the level of this floor, I built a course of dry-stone across the chapel, so that both the clay floor and the original cell front are now visible and should not easily become encumbered again.

There was now the cell itself to excavate, and I have not done this entirely, because at some time the sloping walls have been roughly buttressed on the north and south sides by large stones placed on end. But I have cleared to the paving inside the door, and at the east end I have gone right across the cell. I found an altar of well-built masonry 2 feet 6 inches high, 3 feet broad and 2 feet 3 inches deep. Muir said there was an altar *stone* 3 feet long at the east end of the cell, and he gave a sketch of it in position. Doubtless this was all he could see of the altar at that time, and I found this stone on a level with the top of the altar but at right angles to it. The altar being completely revealed, I replaced the big slab. A visitor to Rona will now get the impression of a simple early church in a very fair state of preservation because it has been almost buried for so long.

Around the chapel is the burial ground, once containing rough stone crosses, and now featuring the modern addition commemmorating the two shepherds, MacDonald and MacKay, who died in 1885.

5 SULASGEIR

ISLAND ROCK

THOUGH often called an island, Sulasgeir is in fact little more than a large sea rock. It is situated in latitude 59° 6′ north and in longitude 6° 10′ west. It is half a mile long (NNE to SSW) and has a maximum breadth of 200 yd. The highest point is 229 ft above sea level and occurs at the extreme southern end of the island. The centre is low and narrow, being only some 20 ft above the waves so that in rough weather the sea breaks completely over the waist of this North Atlantic gannetry. This waist has a sea cave which runs from one side of the island to the other. But this is only one of many caves and geos, for the rock is composed of hornblende gneiss which has been weathered by the constant pounding of waves through the long milleniums since Sulasgeir was first formed. Though but twelve miles or so from its sister island North Rona, to the east, the geology of Sulasgeir is different in some respects. Biotite is present on Sulasgeir as an accessory mineral while it is almost entirely absent from Rona. On the other hand, Rona has more pegmatite veins. On Sulasgeir this mineral is found only in veins which are both small and ill-defined.

There is scarcely any surface soil on Sulasgeir, though some half-dozen species of plants are to be found in rock crevices. These include thrift, scentless mayweed, scurvy grass, orache and chickweed. They occur mostly at the southern end of the island. The northern end is the domain of the seabird population concentrated in a tight-knit ornithopolis.

Sulasgeir is surrounded by satellite islets. The farthest away are Bogha Corr and the larger Gralisgeir, about half a mile to the north-west and south respectively. That all these islets have names indicates that Sulasgeir, though never inhabited for any length of time, has nevertheless been of social and economic

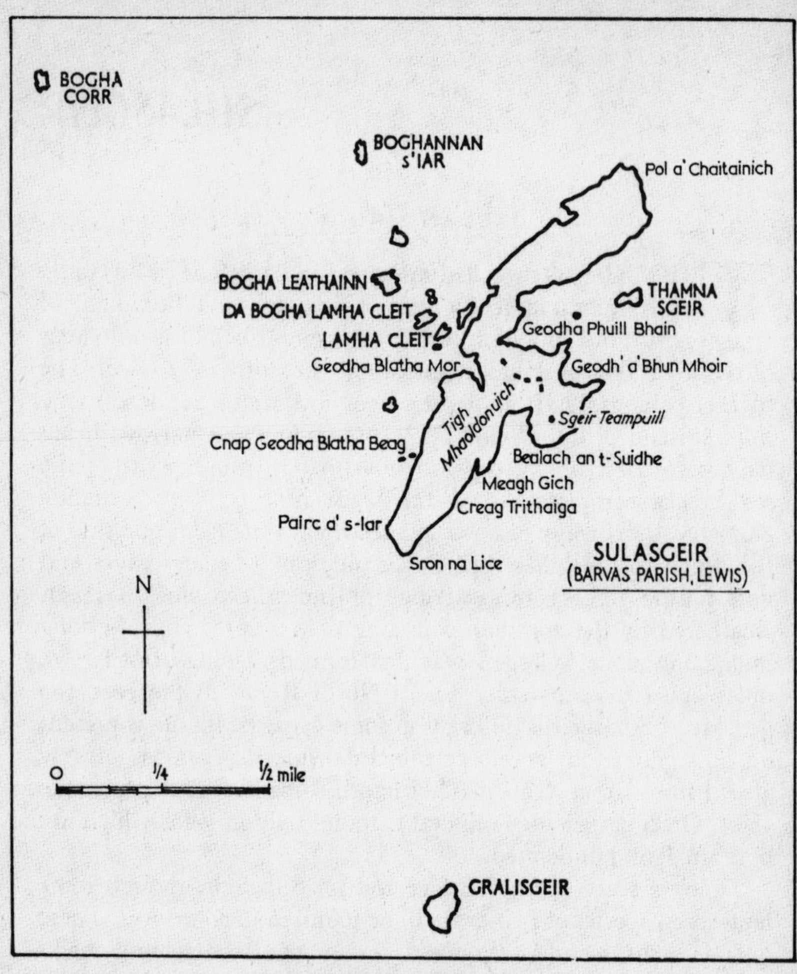

Sketch map of Sulasgeir

importance to the people in the north of the mainland-mass of nearby Lewis.

It is the gannetry on Sulasgeir which has thrown this remote island into far fame and wide recognition, particularly in the world of ornithology. The gannets have in fact given the sea rock the name by which it has been known by Lewismen for centuries: *sula* = solan goose, *sgeir* = rock. It is reckoned that there are some 5,500 pairs on the island. Other birds include guillemots, puffins, Leach's petrel and kittiwakes and fulmars, all of these species breeding in numbers varying from a few hundred to a few thousand.

HISTORY

The inhabitation of Sulasgeir has been only intermittent and brief, a matter of days or a few weeks. In the south part of the island there are some stone bothies and a chapel or cell. The bothies or shelters are all made from dry-stone, built up with large slabs of rock; there is no record as to who constructed them or when they were built. The island has a nature which is so bleak, barren and forbidding that it is almost impossible to imagine any human being electing to live on Sulasgeir—unless an out-and-out hermit. Certainly, since 1549 the island has not been on record as having been inhabited. The bothies were probably erected early in history and kept in good repair at various times through the centuries by the men of Ness, in Lewis, who made annual visits to Sulasgeir for a hunting of gannets, which were used largely for food. T. S. Muir, who visited Sulasgeir in 1860, called one of the bothies a 'chapel'; this structure has a Gaelic name *Tigh Beannaicht*, indicating its religious nature. Muir gives no reason for his making this functional distinction from all the other Sulasgeir bothies. It may be simply that one of the bothies, the 'chapel', was reserved by the visiting men as a meditative sanctuary on the island while the remainder of the buildings were used for secular purposes during the time of their stay catching the young gannets.

There is a tradition in Ness that Sulasgeir was once used as a prison for sheep-stealers. Sheep-stealing was once a crime punishable by death. Life on Sulasgeir was probably regarded in Lewis as a suitable equivalent and perhaps saved the expense of a hangman. Tradition says that farther back in history, *c* AD 500, Sulasgeir was the final prison for Brenhilda, a sister of St Ronan, the patron of nearby North Rona. In yet another small corner of the island's tradition, Sulasgeir is said to have had the honour of being the scene of the first visual contact which Prince Charles Edward had with Scotland and his Scottish clansmen. This happened when his ship was hailed in the vicinity of Sulasgeir by a passing Ness boat-crew making for North Rona.

John Swinburne, who visited Sulasgeir in 1883 to record the birds and the plant species, wrote of a boat-crew of Nessmen from Lewis who were stranded on the island:

> On one occasion now some years ago, a crew from Ness in the Lewis had their boat wrecked in landing on Sula Sgeir in the month of June, and lived on the island for several weeks, sustaining themselves on the flesh of birds. Captain Oliver, who commanded the revenue cruiser, *Prince of Wales*, visited Sula Sgeir in the month of August to look for the lost boat. He found a wreck on it, also an oar on end with an old pair of canvas trousers on it, and, over the remains of a fire, a pot containing bird's flesh; but there being no trace of the men, it was thought that they must have been picked up by a passing vessel. Nothing more was heard of them until the month of October following, when a Russian vessel on her homeward voyage met a Stornoway craft in the Orkneys, and informed the crew of the latter that they had taken the men off Sula Sgeir and landed them in Rona. Captain Oliver at once went to Rona, and found the crew consuming the last barrel of potatoes which the poor shepherd had. He took away the former, and left the latter sufficient provision for the winter.

Sulasgeir, like Rockall, has been the target for gunnery practice through the years. M. Stewart in *Ronay*, published in 1933 says: 'On December 23rd, the 2nd and 4th Battle Squadrons with the *Iron Duke* proceeded to sea to the westward of the Orkneys and carried out target practice at the Sulis-ker rock, north of the Hebrides'. Such is the fate and treatment of lonely sea-islands.

SO THEY SAID OF IT

Through the years, the island has been an attraction for visitors other than the purposeful Nessmen. Each has left a word-picture of Sulasgeir, of his own painting, and often highly stylistic.

One of the first was Dean Monro who paid his visit in 1549. The last in his long list of 251 islands is Sulasgeir:

> Be sixteen mile of sea towards the west of this Ile (North Rona) lyis ane Ile callit Swilskeray, ane mile lang, without girs or hedder, with heich blak craigis and blak fog upon pairt of thame. This Ile is full of wild fowls, and quhan the fowls hes thair birds ripe, men out of the parochin of Niss in Leozus uses to saill thair and tarry 7 or 8 dayis and to fetche with thame hame thair boatful of dry wild fowls with wild fowl fedderis. In this Ile thair hantis ane fowl callit the Colk, little les nor ane goose, quha cummis in vair to the land to 'lay' his eggis and to cleck his birds quhill he bring thame to perfection, and at that time his fleiss of fedderis fallis off him all haillelie, and he flasses to the mayne sea again, and cummis nevir to land quhill the zeiris end again, and than he cummis with his new fleiss of fedderis. This fleiss that he leaves zeirlie upon his nest hes na banes in the fedderis nor any kind of hard thing in thame that may be felt or graipit but utter fine downis.

T. S. Muir in 1860 wrote:

> Sula Sgeir!—the sea-rock of the sulaire or solan goose, I should fancy it means—what can be said of it?—more than it is a high, horrent, and nearly herbless strip of gneiss, or other such-like adamantine matter, scarcely one-third of a mile in extent, and so narrowed in many places that, in the winter-time, the serpent wave must be evermore lashing over from side to side, and cutting up the whole mass into so many the merest of particles?

In June 1887, Harvie-Brown's party of naturalists made a landing on the island from the *Shiantelle*:

> Quite a number of Fulmars were circling round and even resting on the rock, but I searched vainly for eggs or young . . . Foetid hollows and dark-green spray pools . . . usually covered with green slime and feathers, and surrounded by dead young birds, rotten or highly incubated eggs, and old saturated nests . . . Our visit to Sulisgeir in 1887 will ever be remembered as one of the most remarkable incidents of our Hebridean peregrinations during many years, more especially if we look to the

ghastly lonesomeness and geologically disintegrated nature of the whole place; almost pathetically sad in its collection of rough stone huts, the solitary wretched sheep, and the remains of another, and the heads of defunct Gannets strewn all over the surface.

In 1930, Malcolm Stewart, author of *Ronay* visited the island:

Quite apart from the actual buildings, there are to be found a few rusty iron implements—in one of the houses is an empty bottle and a large pot suspended by a chain from the roof, while a piece of old rotten sacking hangs in the doorway. Around are strewn the remains of dead birds. Among the clefts in the cliffs a few old oars and other pieces of wood are to be seen, while near the landing-place is some rusty chain, placed no doubt, to facilitate the hazardous landing. Perhaps the next person to spend a night or two on the island, if anyone might ever wish to do this, will also find in another house a few cans of water, some tinned food, and a spade, and wonder as to how they came there and who brought them.

One who spends a night in or near the bothies of Sula Sgeir will without doubt be rudely awakened by cries and considerable commotion issuing from the walls of the buildings (of Leach's forktail petrel).

John Wilson Dougal, the amateur geologist, whose many visits to Lewis are commemorated in a large white rock on the moor between North Tolsta and Ness, visited Sulasgeir in September 1930:

We were fortunate within ten minutes of landing to discover the abundant presence of Flinty Crush rock . . . The elation of reaching the island—the desire of so many years—helped to sustain us against the soaking showers of rain which beset us as we ranged, hammer in hand, over the rough rocks . . .

Robert Atkinson, an inveterate island-goer, wrote of his landing on Sulasgeir and of a night spent on the island in 1938:

The very ground churned with petrels, they scuttled underfoot, they were headlong in the air . . . The gannets were stilled until we came stumbling along with our torches and disturbed them. The complete changeover of life from day to night was remarkable: all day the sky full of gannets and their unceasing cacophony; a brief no-man's-land of silence at dusk and dawn; all night the wild dashing and outcry of petrels, flying out over the heads of the sleeping gannets.

GANNET HUNTING BY LEWISMEN

Though lying some forty miles from the Butt of Lewis, Sulasgeir had for centuries, but to a lesser degree today, an important rôle in the social and economic life of the Lewis community at Ness. In 1549, as we have seen, Dean Monro referred to the large numbers of sea-fowl on Sulasgeir, and told of the men of Ness who sailed to the island each year for a wild-fowling expedition. The target was the young gannet, or the *guga*, which they caught and killed in their thousands. The *Old Statistical Account of Scotland* (1797) says: 'There is in Ness a most venturous set of people who for a few years back, at the hazard of their lives, went there in an open six-oared boat without even the aid of a compass.' The men stayed on Sulasgeir for about a week and brought back to Lewis a boatful of dried wildfowl and feathers.

The custom of guga-hunting is centuries old and is nowadays characteristic of the Ness district of Lewis and of no other. The reason for this may be that the Ness community has preserved, reasonably intact, the characteristics of their undoubted Norse forebears. Excellent seamanship was certainly essential for the success of the expeditions—rowing across forty miles of turbulent Atlantic water in an open or half-open boat was not a pleasure cruise. To effect a landing with modern boats on Sulasgeir still calls for an exact and detailed knowledge of the island's waters, the currents and the state of the tides. Most of the cliffs on Sulasgeir are high, jagged and sheer. There is only one possible landing place and that is on the east side of the island, at Geodha Phuill Bhain. Even so, the weather must be suitable and the waters reasonably calm before a landing can be effected.

Though it is only the natives of Ness who today regard the guga as a delicacy, in former times the flesh of the young solan goose was widely enjoyed. In the sixteenth century it was served at the table of Scots kings. It found wide favour with the wealthy as a 'whet' or appetiser before meals. This custom is described by John Taylor, the king's Water Poet, in his *Pennyless Pilgrimage* (1618). He says: 'It is very good flesh, but it is eaten in the forme as we eate oysters, standing at the side board, a little before dinner.'

The gannets which provided the flesh for the tables of the Edinburgh elite came from the Bass Rock in the Firth of Forth. About the time Taylor wrote, the birds were 'sold at Edinburgh for twenty pence apiece', a price which, even allowing for the difference in past and present monetary values, compares very favourably with today's charge of about 5s (25p).

By 1938 the bird protectionists had stepped up their shows of disapproval of the Ness hunt. Each year the 2,000 or so dead birds from Sulasgeir brought home by the Nessmen provoked loud cries that this practice would lead to the eventual extinction of the species on Sulasgeir. Both *The Times* and the local newspaper the *Stornoway Gazette* carried solid columns of correspondence, both pro and con. At last the issue reached Parliament and a Question was asked. The 'cons' wanted the Nessmen to stop their voyages altogether. Traditionalists, on the other hand, said that the annual expedition to Sulasgeir was an outward show of the men's daring and enterprise and was a facet of a way of life which was worth preserving, more indeed than a few thousand gannets which were, in any case, a small part of a growing world population of the species. It was also pointed out that commercial gain was not the primary purpose of the Sulasgeir expedition. 2,000 gugas was an average haul; at 1s (5p) per bird the catch was worth £100. This was in fact £10 per man for a fortnight or so of the toughest privation. There were easier ways of making money. The gugas which were not used by the Ness community were sent all over the world to Lewis exiles.

In the end it was inevitable that the gannet should become one of wild birds taken under the protective care of the Protection of Wild Birds Act of 1954. But so strong was the representation on behalf of the Nessmen that a Statutory Order was passed to allow them to perpetuate their tradition and to satisfy their peculiar appetite both for the guga and for adventure.

Mention has already been made of the boat for long used by the

Nessmen to cross forty North Atlantic miles to Sulasgeir. It was the *sco* or *sgoth*. The design was after the style of the Shetland sixern (Old Norse: *sexaeringr*), a clinker-built vessel of fir and fastened with iron. The method of construction was similar to that of the older Viking ships. The overall length was about 30 ft with a keel length of 18–20 ft; the beam varied from 8–10 ft; the hold was some 3 ft deep. The rig consisted of a single square-sail fitted to a mast stepped about amidships. The tack was made fast to the fore-quarter, not to the stem head. The sail had a couple of reefs in the head, and two or three in the foot. The oars were square in the loom. The vessel was undecked, though a half-deck was provided at a later date. The last boat of this type used in Ness was the *Pride of Lionel*, converted to a power boat by the installation of a 7-hp petrol engine.

It was in the *Pride of Lionel* that John Wilson Dougal went to Sulasgeir in 1930 and wrote this account of his voyage in an open boat at night:

> Steadily the boat made its weird passage through the heavy swelling currents . . . In mid-boat the flicker of light from the hand lamp showed the steersman and the crew discussing the course in Gaelic . . . At this stage of night dreaming, when still spelled by the scintillating panorama of the heavens, the boat was dipping and rising from basin to basin, with sometimes a rending slap on the bow that made more than one of us look involuntarily, to see if the bare planks had sprung. There was no pretence that our scow had a trail boat, or even a life-belt.
>
> Forsaking the damp night air, rest was sought for a few hours on a plank and a restless bag of straw, till the grey glimmer of a chilly, sunless morning brought us to look around on the still tossing currents, with early solan geese already alive to the day's necessities . . . Soon we heard with sympathy and interest the skipper's shout, 'Rona, Rona ahead! Sulasgeir! Sulasgeir! Starboard there!' and shaking his fist at the elements of sea and sky, he cried 'Have I not the eye of a hawk?'

After the Second World War, this old type of boat was replaced by a small modern motor-boat. Not that this improvement made the journey less hazardous. Difficulties have been encountered.

SULASGEIR

On the 1952 trip, the gannet hunters suffered a real disaster. The *Mayflower* was lost and the party marooned on the island. They were eventually rescued by the Stornoway lifeboat at great risk to both boat and crew.

Sulasgeir, with its sister island of North Rona, was made a National Nature Reserve in June 1965. Its honorary warden was the late James MacGeoch, of Aviemore, in Inverness-shire, some of whose photographs appear in this book.

6 THE FLANNAN ISLES

THE Flannan Isles, also known as the Seven Hunters, lie in a close group about 20 miles west by north from Gallan Head on the west coast of Lewis. Their latitude is 58° 17′ north; longitude 7° 35′ west. The group contains seven islands worthy of the name and a number of small islets, rocks and reefs. There are three sub-groups: to the north are Eilean Mor and Eilean Tighe; to the south are Soray, Sgeir Toman and Sgeir Righinn; and to the west are Roareim and Eilean a' Ghobha. The Flannans are part of the civil parish of Uig in Lewis. Their total land area is less than 100 acres and they are used only for sheep grazing by Lewis crofters.

The islands are particularly remarkable for the manner in which they rise sheer from the sea. The largest island is Eilean Mor (Big Island) which has a maximum height of 288 ft above sea level. 39 acres in extent, it has a coast line of some 1¼ miles. The next largest island is Eilean Tighe (House Island), with an area of 18 acres. Then follow Eilean a' Ghobha (Smith's Island), Soray, Roareim, Sgeir Toman and Sgeir Righinn with areas of 12, 8, 7, 5, and 3 acres respectively.

All the islands consist of hornblende gneiss with pegmatite veins. The gneiss is rather different from that of North Rona and Sulasgeir in that biotite is more common in the Flannans. The islands, in addition, exhibit a wide geological spectrum. The pegmatite on Eilean Mor shows a rather marked graphic structure. A small tholeiitic dyke has been recorded there. A highly felspathic dyke has been found on Eilean a' Ghobha, of apparently trachytic character. There is a deposit of cemented sand on the top of Roareim.

The largest islands in the group have green grassy tops: 'like a meadow thickly enamelled with daisies' is how Dr MacCulloch described them in 1815. The group supports a large number of birds, particularly seabirds; over one hundred species have been

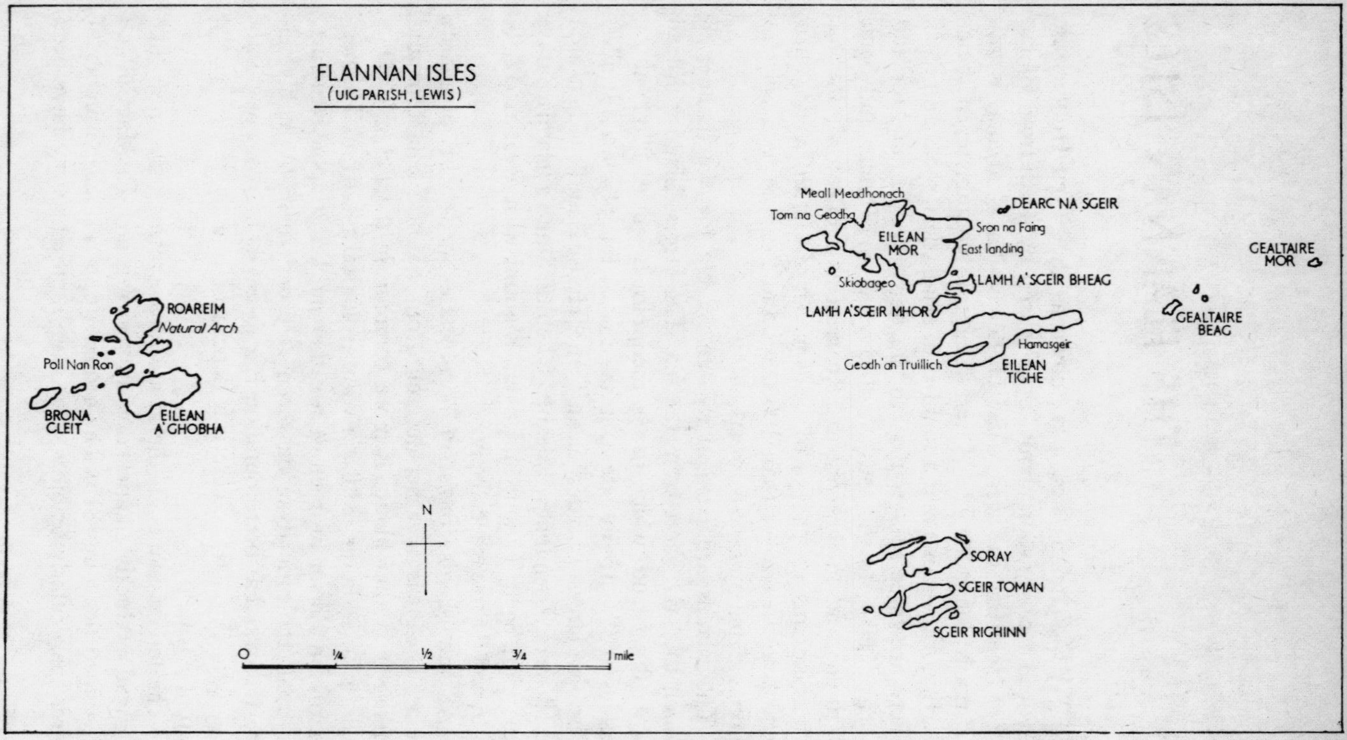

Sketch map of the Flannan Isles

noted. The Flannans are a favourite haunt of *halichaerus grypus*, the grey seal, though it does not breed among the islands.

By far the most important bird is Leach's fork-tailed petrel, which breeds in large numbers in holes in the turf on Eilean Mor. Other birds include the fulmar, shag and the kittiwake. Plant life is sparse and confined largely to those common small flowers associated with isolated maritime lands.

The cliffs on the island are so steep that landing is always extremely difficult and hazardous, and is possible by boat only when the weather is favourable; the swell of the Atlantic waters can easily smash a small boat against the hard and unrelenting rock-faces. One remarkable sight in the Flannans is Brona Cleit, a needle-shaped stack about 100 ft high, at the far end of the western sub-group of islets.

Landing on Eilean Mor, the largest island, is possible at two places. The landings are built up from concrete blocks cemented in place against the cliffs. When the weather prevents an actual boat landing, a crane above each landing-place takes stores, and sometimes men, ashore to the lighthouse from the Northern Lighthouse Board in Edinburgh's supply ship *Pole Star*.

The Flannans Lighthouse is one of a chain of lights in the western approaches of the Atlantic. The structure was built between 1895 and 1899 by D. & C. Stevenson of Edinburgh, the firm of which Robert Louis Stevenson's father was the head. The tower is 75 ft high; the light stands about 330 ft above the sea. It was first lit on 7 December 1899. A framed notice in the tower of the lighthouse reads:

> The Commissioners of Northern Lighthouses hereby give notice that on the night of Thursday the 7th day of December next, and every evening thereafter, a light will be exhibited from the lighthouse which has been erected on Eilean Mor, one of the Flannan Islands. The light will be a group flashing White Light showing 2 flashes in quick succession every half minute. The power of the light will be equal to about 140,000 standard candles. The Light will be visible all around and will be elevated 330 feet above high water spring tides, and allowing fifteen feet for the height of the eye will be seen at about 24 nautical miles in clear weather, and at lesser distances accord-

ing to the state of the atmosphere. When close to, the stacks lying to the westward of Eilean Mor will obscure the Light over two small angles. The top of the lantern is about 75 feet above the island.

By order of the Board

Edinburgh, 30 Oct. 1899 James Murdoch Secretary.

The Flannan's Light is one of the world's remotest lighthouses. In 1971 the light became 'automatic' and is now monitored by radio from the Butt of Lewis lighthouse, thirty-five miles away. As well as enabling the supervising keepers to check that the light is functioning, the monitor indicates which of the four gas mantles is in use; when the gas pressure falls below the safe limit a signal is sent to the Butt. The range of the Flannans light is 25 nautical miles.

THE ROLE OF MAN

The Flannan Isles have always played an important part in the ecology of the folk of Lewis in that they offered both grazing for sheep and the chance to obtain substantial supplies of bird-oil, bird-flesh and feathers, not to mention birds' eggs to add a tasty supplement to a normally monotonous diet.

The island group supposedly takes its name Flannan from one of two saints. There was Flannan, once Bishop of Cell da Lua (Killaloe) on Lough Derg on the River Shannon in Eire. An account of this Flannan is given in the Irish Book of Leinster. He was possibly a contemporary of St Brendan, the Irish sailor-saint. Flannan was of royal blood. His father had been king of the Dal gGais and retired late in life to become a monk at Lismore. His influence on his son was considerable. There is some rather slight evidence that this Flannan preached in Scotland. If this is true then he is an obvious candidate for consideration for the honour of the derivation of the name of the island-group. The alternative is St Flann, the son of Maol-duine, Abbot of Iona who died in AD 891.

Whichever it was, indeed if ever any saintly seafaring missionary landed on the islands, the Flannans have had for centuries a very strong religious association, more so than any of the other Hebridean islands and islets remote from land. It may have been the awe-inspiring sight and appearance of the cliffs, with their teeming birds and their startling suddenness as they rise out of the sea, miles from land, that gave them their 'atmosphere', so much related to the highly elevated spiritual plane on which the Celtic mind often operates.

Eilean Mor carries the inevitable chapel, dedicated to St Flannan and surrounded by a host of taboos originated and perpetuated by many generations of visiting Lewismen. The chapel or cell is built of dry stone. It is called Teampull Beannachadh, or Blessing House. Its internal measurements are 5 ft x 7¾ ft. The walls average 30 in thick; at the gables the roof rises to about 9 ft; there is a small, low doorway in the west end. The building is situated near the lighthouse. T. S. Muir said of it: '. . . a very primitive-looking thing, composed of rough stones joggled compactly together'.

Towards the western end of Eilean Mor are the Bothies of the Clan MacPhail (Bothan Clann 'IcPhail). These are also stone-built in much the same style as the temple. In all probability these structures housed the men from Lewis when they visited the islands. Eilean Tighe gets its name from the 'house' which according to Malcolm Stewart (who landed there in 1932) was 'a collection of stones arranged in an oval to round formation'.

Three writers have passed on good descriptions of the Flannan Isles. The first is Dean Monro who wrote in 1549:

> Seven Haley Isles. First, furth 50 myle in the Occident seas from the coste of the parochin Vye in Lewis, towarts the west northwest, lyes the seven iles of Flanayn, claid with girth, and Haley Isles, verey natural gressing within thir saids iles; infinit wyld scheipe therein, quhilk na man knawes to quhom the said sheipe apperteines within them that lives this day of the countrymen; bot M'Cloyd of the Lewis, at certaine tymes in the zeir, sendis men in, and huntis and slayis maney of thir sheipe. The fleshche of thir sheipe cannot be eaten be honest men for fatnesse, for ther is na flesche on them, bot all quhyte lyke talloune, and it is verey wyld gusted lykways. The saids iles are nouder manurit nor inhabit, bot full of grein high hills, full of wyld sheipe in the seven iles forsaid, quhilk may not be outrune. They pertaine to M'Cloyd of the Lewis.

The next account is written by John Morison, a Harrisman domiciled in Lewis who left a large number of MSS on Lewis history and traditions. He writes *c* 1688 :

> There are seven Islands 15 myles Westward from the Lews, called the Isle of Sant Flannan, lying closs together; wherin there a cheaple, where Sant Flandan himself lived ane heremit. To those in summertyme some countriemen goes; and bringeth home great store of seafouls and feathers. They way they kill the fowls is, one goeth and taketh a road 10 or 12 foot long, and setts his back to a rock or craig, and as the fouls flieth by, he smitheth them continuallie, and he hes ane other attending to catch all that falls to the ground; for the fouls flee there so thick that those who are beneath them cannot see the firmament. These Isles are not inhabited, but containeth a quantitie of wilde sheep verie fatt and weel fleeced.
>
> When the people goe there, they use everie two men to be Comerads. They hold it a breach of the sanctitie of the place (for they count it holier than anie other) if any man take a drink of water unknown to his comerade or eat ane egg or legg of ane foull, yea take a snuff if tobacco : It is for centaintie that upon a tyme a Countriefellow being sent there and left in it, be reason he could not be keept from theft and robberie and so on a time the fire went out with him, without which he could not live, and so despaired of lyfe and since he saw that there was no remead, he betook him to pray both to God and the Sainct of the Island as they term'd it and by night being fallen in a deep sleep, he sees a man come to him well clade saying aryse, betake thee unto the Altar and there thou shall find a peate in fyre, for the Lord hath heard they prayer. So he arose and accordingly found the fyre, which he preserved untill he was taken home, and henceforth he proved as honest a man as was in the Countrie.

The third description of the island-group comes from Martin Martin (1697). His account details the superstitions of the bird-fowlers who visited the islands :

> To the north-west of Gallan-head, and within six leagues of it lie the Flannan-Islands, which the seamen call North-hunters; they are but small islands, and six in number, and maintain about seventy sheep yearly. The inhabitants of the

adjacent lands of the Lewis, having a right to these islands, visit them once every summer, and there make a great purchase of fowls, eggs, down, feathers, and quills. When they go to sea, they have their boat well manned, and make towards the islands in an east wind; but if before, or at landing, the wind turn westerly, they hoist up sail, and steer directly home again. If any of their crew is a novice, and not versed in the customs of the place, he must be instructed perfectly in all the punctilloes observed here before landing; and to prevent inconveniences that they think may ensue upon the transgression of the least nicety observed here, every novice is joined with another, that can instruct him all the time of their fowling: so that all the boat's crew are matched in this manner.

After their landing, they fasten the boat to the sides of a rock, and then fix a wooden ladder, by laying a stone at the foot of it, to prevent its falling into the sea; and when they are got up into the island, all of them uncover their heads, and make a turn sun-ways round, thanking God for their safety. The first injunction given after landing, is not to ease nature in that place where the boat lies, for that they reckon a crime of the highest nature, and of dangerous consequence to all their crew; for they have a great regard to that very piece of rock upon which they first set their feet, after escaping the danger of the ocean.

The biggest of these islands is called Island-More; it has the ruins of a chapel dedicated to St Flannan, from whom the island derives its name. When they are come within about 20 paces of the altar, they all strip themselves of their upper garments at once; and their upper clothes being laid on a stone, which stands there on purpose for that use, all the crew pray three times before they begin fowling: the first day they say the first prayer, advancing towards the chapel upon their knees; the second prayer is said as they go round the chapel; the third is said hard by or at the chapel; and this is their morning service. Their vespers are performed with the like number of prayers. Another rule is that it is absolutely unlawful to kill a fowl with a stone, for that they reckon a great barbarity, and directly contrary to ancient custom.

It is also unlawful to kill a fowl before they ascend by the ladder. It is absolutely unlawful to call the island of St Kilda (which lies thirty leagues southward) by its proper Irish name

Hirt, but only the high country. They must not so much as once name the islands in which they are following by the ordinary name Flannan, but only the country. There are several other things that must not be called by their common names, e.g., Visk, which in the language of the natives signifies Water, they call Burn; a Rock, which in their language is Creg, must here be called Cruey, i.e., hard; Shore in their language, expressed by Claddach, must here be called Vah, i.e. a Cave; Sour in their language is expressed Gort, but must here be called Gaire, i.e., sharp; Slippery, which is expressed Bog, must be called Soft; and several other things to this purpose. They account it also unlawful to kill a fowl after evening-prayers. There is an ancient custom by which the crew is obliged not to carry home any sheep-suet, let them kill ever so many sheep in these islands. One of their principal customs is not to steal or eat anything unknown to their partner, else a transgressor (they say) will certainly vomit it up; which they reckon a just judgment. When they have loaded their boat sufficiently with sheep, fowls, eggs, down, fish &c., they make the best of their way homeward. It is observed of the sheep of these islands that they are exceeding fat, and have long horns.

I had this superstitious account not only from several of the natives of the Lewis, but likewise from two who had been in the Flannan Islands the preceding year. I asked one of them if he prayed at home as often, and as fervently as he did when in the Flannan Islands; and he plainly confessed to me that he did not: adding further, that these remote Islands were places of inherent sanctity; and that there was none ever yet landed in them but found himself more disposed to devotion there, than anywhere else.

THE FLANNAN'S MYSTERY

For centuries the sea has been the sole possessor of clues to the many unsolved mysteries, strange happenings, baffling phenomena which have taken place on the surface of its waters. On a par with the mystery of the *Marie Celeste*, the complete and utter disappearance of three keepers from the lighthouse on Eilean Mor in December 1900 has been, and still is, a matter for new theories to account for the happening.

On 15 December 1900, the steamer *Archer*, bound from Philadelphia to Leith, passed within a few miles of the island group. Though the black masses of the islands were clearly visible in the moonlight, there was no beam from the lantern on Eilean Mor. The skipper of the *Archer* reported his discovery when he made landing at Oban. A message was sent to the Northern Lighthouse Board relief ship, *Hesperus*, which was anchored in Little Loch Roag. But before she could venture out to investigate the happening, a series of strong gales blew up and it was not until 26 December that she was able to make steam for the Flannans.

When the *Hesperus* reached the Flannans she signalled her arrival by whistle, then by rocket. From her position at the east landing she could see the lighthouse buildings. But there was no flag signal from the flagstaff, nor were there the normal signs of activity which usually accompanied the arrival of the ship. A boat was lowered and a party went ashore. At the jetty, the first sign was noticed that something was amiss. Normally, it would have been piled with empty provision boxes for return to the shore base. Now it was bare.

In a mounting fit of alarm, the party, which included Joseph Moore, a relief keeper, climbed up the concrete steps and ran up over the inclined path over the brow of the cliff to the lighthouse. There was an uncanny silence which was accentuated when they entered the living-room. The fire was dead. The clock had stopped. On the table lay a meal which had never even been touched. There was cold meat, pickles and a dish of potatoes. An overturned chair lay a silent witness on the floor. The men then went up the spiral steps to the sleeping quarters. There they found the beds, made up in the clean, clinical way of sailors. In the galley, pots, pans and dishes sparkled. Moore went up to the lantern room. He found the lamp cold. The wicks had been trimmed and the lenses were polished clean. All was operational in fact. There was absolutely no reason for the lamp being out.

After a further search the logbook of the chief keeper, Ducat, was found. The entries were made up to 13 December. A slate was discovered which took the record to 9 o'clock on the morning of 15 December. The entries told of weather conditions and the state of the lantern, that there had been gales and heavy seas for a week and that there was evidence of severe damage at the west landing which had been reduced to a shambles. A crane, which had been set fast in a bed of concrete some 100 ft above the high-water mark, had been torn from its fixings. A concrete rope box about 40 ft higher up had also been torn away and smashed to pieces. Heavy iron stanchions on the concrete stairs were twisted. And for about thirty feet along the top of the cliff, standing 200 ft above high-water mark, the turf had been torn away. A boulder weighing nearly a ton had been wrested from its centuries-old bed and rolled a considerable distance. Obviously the storm had been unusually severe. But the keepers had survived it and the last entry on the slate made by Principal Ducat was that the wind was moderating.

A search carried on outside the lighthouse revealed no sign of the keepers. Nothing was found which could account for the disappearance of the three men.

The mystery was heightened by the fact that both Ducat's and Marshall's oilskins and seaboots were missing. Only MacArthur's clothes and boots could be found.

A full-scale official investigation was begun. Some facts emerged from the inquiry. One was that the oilskins and seaboots were used by the keepers only when visiting one or other of the landings. The other was that the east landing was in good order while the west was in bad need of reconstruction and repair. In the end, no definite conclusion was reached as to the explanation of the disappearance of the three men. 'It is to be assumed', concluded the Report, 'that the three men, for some reason, left their post, were caught by an unexpected heavy sea and drowned.'

The nearest explanation of the mystery comes from local knowledge of the sea conditions which sometimes exist round the Flannans, conditions which men in their first year on the island of Eilean Mor could not be expected to know. This theory also accounts for the damage done to the west landing. After severe storms in the Atlantic, huge isolated waves come rolling in on the islands to dash against the rock-cliffs. The rebound waves are often more violent than the original or parent wave.

The west landing on Eilean Mor is in an inlet called Skiopageo.

It is a few hundred yards long and ends in a cave which at high tide can be closed completely. In certain conditions of high storm, wave upon wave of water is pushed into the cave. The pressure of the resident air is thus built up to such an extent that it eventually explodes outwards and tons of water fall onto the adjacent sides of the geo or gully, including the west jetty.

The theory about the Flannans' mystery is that after the storm-damage to the west landing, two of the keepers, Ducat and Marshall, went down to the landing wearing their outdoor clothes and boots. As they were experienced seamen, though not local men, they well knew to keep an eye to seaward for incoming waves. One such wave might well have swept into the geo, followed by smaller waves to begin the build-up of pressure inside the cave. In the meantime, MacArthur, the third keeper, was probably in the lighthouse and setting the last touches to the breakfast table. A glance out to sea would be sufficient to notice an incoming wave of more than usual height making for the west of the island with its attendant follower waves. Being a local man, he realised the importance of warning his mates. He rushed to the door, knocked over a chair, and, forsaking his oilskins and boots, ran to the west landing calling out to watch for the wave which would rebound on them. He then might well have had to descend to the jetty to make himself understood and in the meantime died with his fellow keepers as the Skiopageo cave exploded to disgorge its death-wall of sea water onto the unfortunate men.

It will never be known for certain just what happened. One can in these matters come only as close to the truth as the human imagination will allow. But the mystery still remains unsolved, like a haunting, unexorcised cloud hovering over the Seven Hunters. One cannot visit Eilean Mor, look far-down at the heaving, white-capped waves beneath and not feel that little bit unnerved at something which lies just outside the pale of human knowledge and understanding.

PERSONAL NOTE

Wilfred William Gibson's poem was almost a set piece for learning in the Nicolson Institute, Stornoway, where the present author schooled. The subject of the poem was the mystery of the Flannans and the disappearance of the three lighthouse keepers. In particular, the last couplet almost rang a knell of fear through us as we recited 'Three men alive on Flannan Isle, who thought, on three men dead.' The mystery was heightened by the knowledge that the islands were remote and might have been well beyond the edge of the world so far as accessibility was concerned. But one day a visit was made possible for the author, a visit still remembered clearly after more than two decades.

The chance came when a holiday was being spent at the Lighthouse Shore Station at Breascleit. The relief ship *Pole Star* was due to visit the Flannans and casual labour was needed to offload stores from the ship's small boat. Though there was hard work involved, the pay was 30s (£1·50) for the day's trip and in addition, the greater reward, the opportunity of becoming a visitor to these remote Atlantic islands.

We left the jetty at Breascleit, in Little Loch Roag, and boarded the *Pole Star* anchored off-shore. In the early morning light any other journey would have had dull prospects, but the excitement of a visit to the Flannans was hard to suppress. The voyage took over two hours. First sighting of the islands was spots, like thick dark clouds, low on the far horizon. Then they solidified, took shape, and rose to their full height out of the sea. The islands were almost like growths speeded up by camera. Soon they were towering above the ship. The immediate impact was one of foreboding and a sense of physical inferiority as we had to crick our necks to view the lighthouse perched on top of Eilean Mor against a moving backcloth of clouds. Birds showered themselves round the cliff faces in their thousands. And at the cliff-roots, seals slithered off the seaweed-covered slippery rocks as the *Pole Star* blew her hooter. The sound echoed above the ship and bounced itself off the surrounding islands before it died away in a series of half echoes, which served only to emphasise the loneliness of the Flannans.

The small boat was lowered and we made for the south landing. From sea level, Eilean Mor looked like a low-backed whale rising from the sea. A jump onto slippery, wet sea-smelling rock and one was ashore, clinging to iron rungs wedded firmly to the rock face and climbing up the 160 steps to the top. The landings on Eilean Mor are so placed that one of them can be used for boat, or if necessary crane landing, at any time of the year, depending on the prevailing weather conditions. From each landing there is a small rail-track on which runs a trolley operated by a cable wound up by a drum in the engine-shed beside the lighthouse. The rails from each landing meet at 'Charing Cross' to form a single line up to the lighthouse. The lighthouse itself consists of a white tower and lantern. The surrounding walled building comprises the stores and living quarters of the keepers.

As the youngest member of the labour squad, I was excused much of the work involved in landing the stores, oil drums and coal, and was offered the chance, eagerly taken, of being shown round the light. The recollection is still clear of clinical cleanliness, polished warm-looking brasses and copper pipes and a pleasant whiteness. From the tower, the view of the other islands in the Flannans group seemed unreal. This was probably a natural reaction. Land-based humans become so accustomed to assessing the sea in terms of land, that when the land is secondary in importance to a vast acreage of sea, it takes a considerable mental adjustment to realise that in certain vistas it is the sea which provides the dominant and over-riding characteristic, and which makes any solid mass, a small island in particular, seem an intruder.

It was not a long visit. The hours passed too quickly and it was soon time to leave Eilean Mor. But not without a large quantity of gulls eggs to take home for a breakfast, and some blown eggs (given by the keepers) as souvenirs. These eggs had a combination taste of egg yolk and fish. One egg was big enough to fill a frying pan. As the year was 1945, and rationing was still in force, the salty taste of the eggs was no barrier to a full appreciation of the nourishment they yielded.

The voyage back was marked by another event. Lunching in the galley of the *Pole Star*, we listened to the news on the radio. The announcer, in unfeeling tones, told us that within the previous twenty-four hours, an atomic bomb had been dropped on Japan, with appalling injury and loss of life. Though none of us really understood the full impact of the news, there was the general undefined feeling that we had suddenly been pushed without warning into a new age with new and unknown horizons, possibly resulting in lighthouses becoming anachronisms and the Flannans group of Hebridean outliers becoming completely deserted by humans, however functional their present stay on Eilean Mor.

7 THE MONACH ISLES AND HEISGEIR ROCKS

THE MONACH ISLES

THE Monach group of low-lying islands is some 8 miles south-west of Hougharry Point in North Uist. Though they are relatively near the large island-mass of North Uist, the islands are somewhat inaccessible and are truly oceanic islands, being completely exposed to the full advances of the Atlantic. The group consists of five islands, three of which are joined together at low tide, like Siamese triplets, by exposed, shallow, sandy beaches. The three main islands are Ceann Ear (East Head), Shivinish, and Ceann Iar (West Head). The two other smaller islands are Sillay, the site of a now-deserted lighthouse, and Stogay. The total area is some 600 acres, most of which is now used for grazing sheep.

The islands are less than 50 ft above sea level, and in this respect they differ from other island subjects of this book. They are basically Lewisian gneiss covered with sand-dunes or machar and protected by reefs. Despite the lack of adequate protection, usually offered by high hills and cliffs on other islands, the Monach Isles have a long history of human settlement.

The plant life on these islands is typical of the sandy-soil covering or machar associated with much of the Outer Hebrides. This soil, based on fertile shell-sand, generates a thick, springy turf which supports a wide variety of flowers. These include stonecrop, kidney-vetch, thyme, heartsease and bird's-foot trefoil. Marram grass is a particular feature, being used to keep the sand dunes in control by stabilising them. Otherwise, as occurred in 1810, the sand becomes exposed to high winds and generations of work to keep the topsoil intact disappear overnight. Seabirds are not so plentiful on these islands because of the lack of cliff-

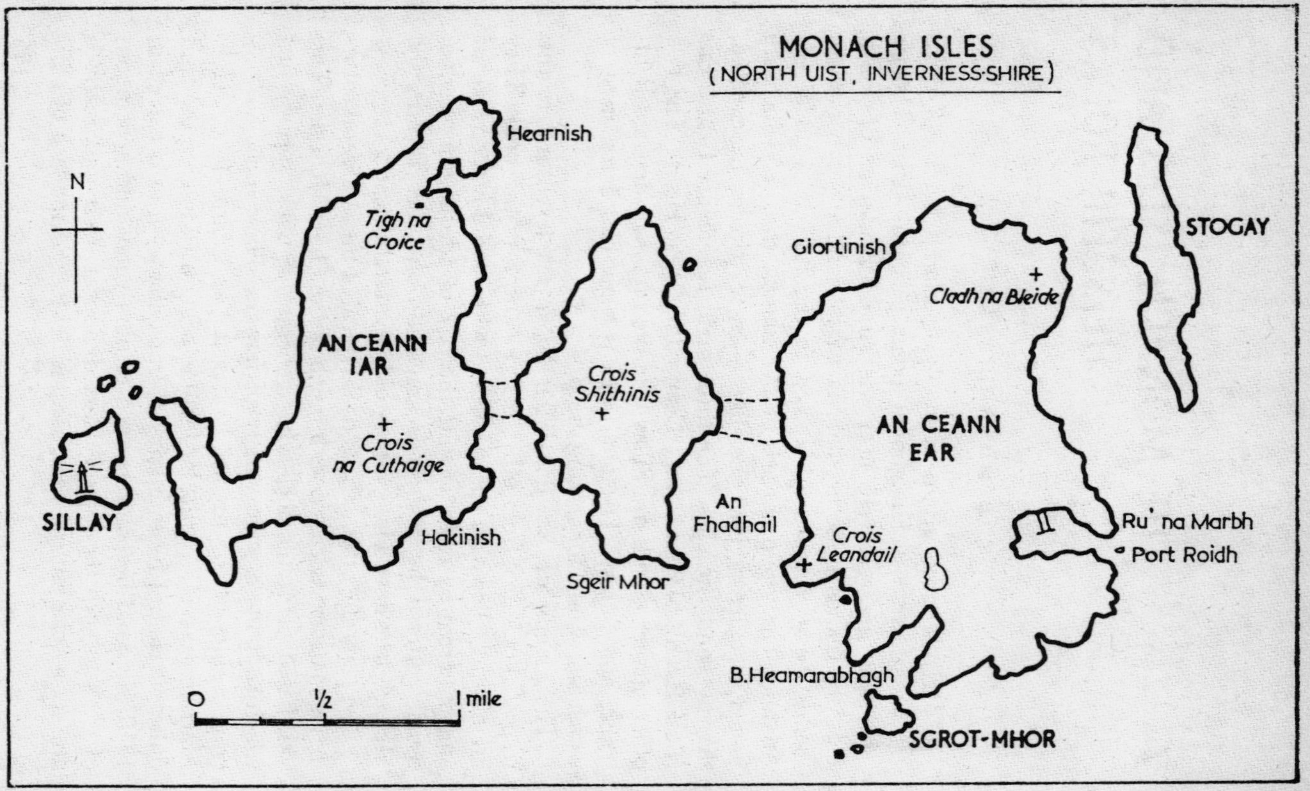

Sketch map of the Monach Isles

shelter. Some birds, however, like arctic terns, make their nests in scoops in the sand.

History

> Be aucht mile of sea from this Ile (Uist) towards the west lyis and Ile four mile lang, half mile braid, laich mane lane, callit Helsker na Caillach, pertaining to the Nunnis of Colmkill, gude corn land not well fyrit.

Thus Dean Monro describes, *c* 1549, the Monach Isles group. But long before the dean visited the Outer Hebrides, the isles were well-known. As far back in history as 1263, the year of the Battle of Largs, the islands were significant as places which yielded a good living for a large number of people. The early visiting Norsemen gave many of the island's reefs and skerries Norse-derived names; the Gaelic element in the placenames of these islands is small.

One of the earliest references to the islands is in connection with the establishment of a nunnery attached to Iona. The nunnery was set up on Ceann Ear, the most easterly island of the interconnected group. It is said of these nuns that they were so strong as to be able to handle large boats which they rowed across the Sound of Monach to North Uist, returning with loads of peat for fuel, which the island-group has always lacked.

The Norse name for the island-group was Heisgeir. But the association of the islands with a male monastery set up on Sillay, the westerly isolated island of the group, caused the name to be changed to Monach. It was part of the monks' duties to maintain a light on Sillay to act as a navigational guide to mariners sailing in the nearby western Atlantic waters. This light is supposed to have been sited on a rock, or altar. The religious associations came to an end after the Reformation.

The first recorded owner of the Monach group was Ailean MacRuairi 'ic Shomhairle, who also possessed Uist. He had connections with the dynasty of the Lords of the Isles. Much later (1644) the ownership fell into the hands of Lord James MacDonald of Sleat in Skye. In 1856 these MacDonalds sold Uist and the Monach Islands to Major Iain P. Orde who passed over his property to the Duke of Hamilton in 1944. The present owner is Lord Granville, the Queen's cousin.

In 1595 the islands were said to be able to raise twenty men of military age, suggesting a total population of some hundred people. In 1764 John Walker recorded a population of seventy. That the islands were surprisingly fertile is indicated in records of *c* 1800 which estimated that some 1,000 cattle were being carried. Six years earlier the Rev Allan MacQueen had written: 'The soil is sandy, yields very little grass at any time, and is only valuable on account of its kelp shores and a small quantity of grain it produces.' But, despite MacQueen's report, there must have been sufficient produce to feed a large community with some to spare. For, a century before, in 1692, a shipload of meal was sent from Heisgeir to Ballachulish for the islanders' kinsmen, the MacDonalds of Glencoe, soon after that clan had suffered the dreadful atrocity known as the Massacre of Glencoe.

In 1810 or thereabouts, however, the population of the islands was almost entirely removed. The reason for the sudden exodus was the complete failure of the soil. The records point to overgrazing, which exposed large areas of sand. This erosion was coupled with a great storm which tore up the turf and covered the islands with still more sand. In an attempt to reclaim the land, sea-bent or marram grass was planted and in time the land recovered sufficiently to support a population again. By 1841 there were two farmers with their families, a female weaver and a herd, totalling 19 people. By 1861 this number had increased to 127, which included some visiting lobster fishermen from Ireland and Islay. In 1891 the maximum population of 135 was recorded. This figure included the native residents, twelve lighthouse keepers and their families and some twelve visiting fishermen.

There were ten crofts sharing 141 acres of runrig arable land and about 400 acres of pasture. These crofts also had a share of the common grazing grounds on North Uist where they also held a common croft; this gave them the necessary elegibility qualification to participate in the North Uist land.

After the turn of this century the population began to fall. In 1914 there were twelve families, probably about eighty persons; in 1921 the population numbered sixty-six. Ten years later it was thirty-three. The following year saw only two families on the Monach Isles and they left in 1942. The 1951 census showed the islands deserted.

In the old tradition of the monks who lived on Sillay, and who had felt it part of their duty to their fellow-men to warn sailors of the dangerous reefs round the islands, a lighthouse was erected on Sillay in 1864. It was 135 ft high and had a range of 18 miles. Tradition has it that this light was built on the same spot as the ancient altar which was provided with a continuous fire beacon. However, sea disasters did occur despite the Sillay light, which often failed to penetrate through the dense sea fogs. In 1894 the *Inflexible* from Sunderland was wrecked on the reef of Sgeir Mhor Shithinis. This was an ill wind which blew good for the islanders for the wreck provided them with some necessary and much-needed materials. In 1903 the *Vanstable* of Dunkirk struck the hard teeth of the Diurabergs, six miles north of the Sillay light. Again, the islanders found cause to bless the storms which brought such bounty to their shores.

The Gulf Stream also brought the islanders wealth. In fact, records indicate that the amount of wreckage thrown up on the shores of the Monach Isles was so great and such a source of profit that the islanders were relatively rich.

The Sillay light was extinguished in 1942, during the Second World War, and has been permanently discontinued. The lighthouse keepers and their families were the last residents of the Monach Isles. In the winter months of 1936, two of the lighthouse keepers were drowned when the small boat in which they were returning from Ceann Ear to Sillay with mails was overtaken by heavy seas. A third keeper watched the tragedy from the lighthouse helpless to do anything for his fellow keepers.

The island community was well served with amenities provided by various agencies. There was a Post Office, though no shop. A Ladies' Highland Association school was provided on the island. Later the Free Church manned the school. After 1874 the school was operated by the School Board. For many years there was in addition a missionary and mision-church of the Glasgow and West Coast Mission. In 1876, a formal missionary appointment was made, the appointee having already devoted twenty-eight years to the satisfaction of the spiritual needs of the Monach community. His official recognition meant full employment for three days each week for a salary of £20 per annum. He held the post for another thirty years after which he was succeeded by his son.

The Monach Isles are now only occasionally populated by lobster fishermen who visit the islands and lodge in the houses which still remain in a reasonable state of repair.

THE HEISGEIR ROCKS

About twelve miles to the north of the Monach Isles lie the Heisgeir Rocks. Heisgeir Eagach has no vegetation. The main islet, Heisgeir Mhor, has about 4 acres of coarse grass and vegetation. Dean Monro, 1549, says:

> To the north-west of the Keantuach of Vyist lyis ane Ile be 12 mile of sea callit Haifsker, quhairin infinite slauchter of selchis is maid at certane times in the zeir . . .

Martin Martin, 1695, says of the islets:

> About three leagues and a half to the West, lie the small Islands called Hawsker-Rocks, and Hawsker-Eggath, and Hawsker-Nimannich, id est, Monk's-Rock, which hath an Altar in it, the first so called from the Ocean as being near to it, for Haw or Thau in the Ancient Language signifies the Ocean: the more Southerly Rocks are six or seven big ones, nicked or indented, for Eggath signifies so much. The largest island, which is Northward, is near half a mile in Circumference, and it is covered with long Grass. Only small Vessels can pass between this and the Southern Rocks, being nearest to St Kilda of all the West Islands; both of 'em abound with Fowls, as much as any Isles of their extent in St Kilda. The Coulterneb, Guillemot, and Scarts are most numerous here, the Seals likewise abound very much in and about these rocks.

As Martin says, these rocks have ever been a favourite haunt of the Atlantic seals. The islets have never supported a human population, but, because of the economic value of the seals, have been a significant factor in the economy of neighbouring Uist.

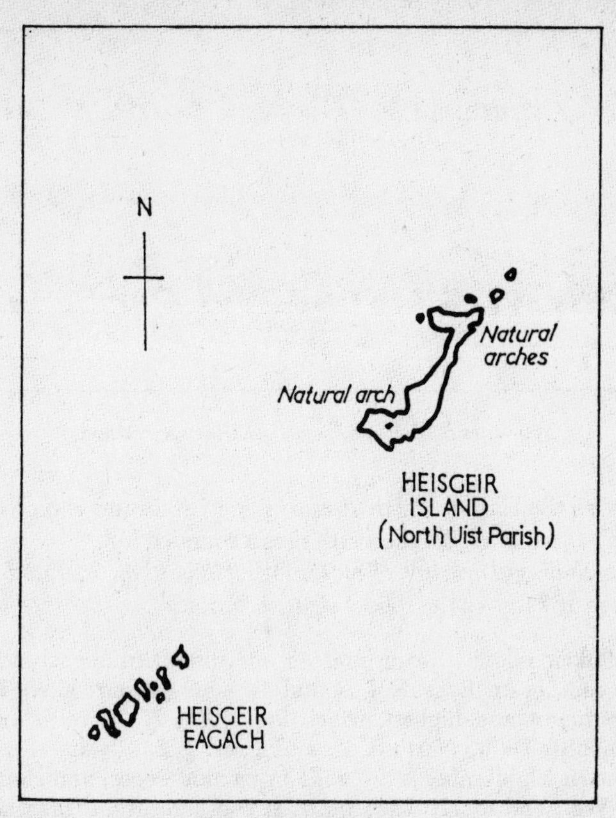

Sketch map of Heisgeir

The slaughter of the seals on Heisgeir has attracted much comment over the years. Visits were paid to the breeding grounds shortly after the cow seals had calved and indiscriminate clubbing took place. There was a complete lack of any sense of conservation. By an Act of Parliament, passed in 1931, the killing of grey seals at any season of the year at this island group is illegal. Heisgeir is now their sanctuary.

Heisgeir Eagach really consists of five distinct islets or stacks which rise close together with deep-water channels of the Atlantic flowing between them. On Heisgeir Mhor, the lowest land lies at the centre of the islet. At the north is the high sea cliff known

Outlines of Heisgeir Eagach and Heisgeir Island

locally as the Castle, which rises to some 120 ft and is pierced by an arch at sea level. To the south rises a rounded hill.

The *Sailing Directions for the West Coast of Scotland* published in 1874 gives the following description:

> Haskeir islands, two in number, are distant from each other one mile in an E by N ¼ N and W by S ¼ S direction, The easternmost and highest, which lies NW ⅓ N, 6½ miles from Griminish Point, North Uist, and NNE ½ E, 10⅓ miles from Monach Lighthouse, is one mile in circumference, and rises at the West end to 120 feet; the East end is nearly as high, and between the two the land is very low and nearly divided by a remarkable cave or basin, 140 feet long and 34 feet broad, so that from a distance of 5 or 6 miles the island shews two flattish lumps. Towards the West end are 3 or four acres of rich soil and coarse grass, but in winter the waves cast their spray over the whole surface; no springs could be found, but there are several pools with brackish water, where the Seals resort in autumn with their young. Rocks dry half a cable off the West and South-West points, but the East side is bold-to: the best landing is on the North and South side of the East lump according to the wind, but it can only be effected with safety during fine weather.
>
> Haskeir Aag, the western of the two islands, may be said to be composed of five bare rocks, with deep water channels be-

tween; they are without a blade of grass or any fresh water, and can only be landed on in fine weather. The highest is 83 feet above the sea.

Other sundry reefs and rocks are indicated on the admiralty chart for the area. There is no anchorage in the vicinity.

APPENDIX A

NATURAL HISTORY

GENERAL DESCRIPTION

ISLANDS, particularly oceanic islands, provide the biologist with fields of immense significance for plant and animal life. In particular, such islands have played, and continue to play, a crucial role in the survival of species of migrant and semi-migrant fauna. St Kilda, now that it has been deserted for almost half a century, offers one of the most interesting subjects in Britain for the student of natural history.

For obvious reasons, the flora and fauna of the Hebridean outliers are limited in their range. The flora of North Rona, for instance, contains as few as forty-one species; and some of these, such as the curled dock (*rumex crispus*) are cliff-dwellers brought to the island by migrant birds. On Sulasgeir, a dozen or so miles from North Rona, there are only seven plant species. The Flannans have twenty-two species and St Kilda, as might be expected, offers the greatest variety with some 140 species. The fauna of the islands can be said to be incidental, except those species such as the Soay sheep, the St Kilda wren and field mouse, and the Atlantic grey seal. The latter mammal is the rarest of the world's total of twenty-five seal species; it congregates at North Rona in larger numbers than anywhere else. Of course, there are numerous seabirds, in particular Leach's petrel.

The St Kilda group of Hebridean Outliers, being the largest of Hebridean sub-oceanic islands, has an interesting variety of flora and fauna, though the latter is mainly confined to birds. In addition, there are individual showings of particular interest. It has been suggested that the escape of the islands from the overall pleistocene glaciation resulted in the survival of certain species of flowers, such as the honeysuckle, vetch and lesser celandine, as remnants of a past woodland flora. These, however may well have been introduced by migrant birds or human agencies.

The following list of plant species recorded on North Rona in 1939 is from Atkinson, *Island Going.*

Lesser spearwort	*Ranunculus flammula*
Creeping buttercup	*Ranunculus repens*
Scurvy grass	*Cochlearia officinalis*
Sea pearlwort	*Sagina maritima*
Mouse-ear chickweed	*Cerastium triviale*
Chickweed	*Stellaria media*
Water chickweed	*Montia fontana*
Wild white clover	*Trifolium repens*
Silverweed	*Potentilla anserina*
Marsh pennywort	*Hydocotyle vulgaris*
Lovage	*Ligusticum scoticum*
Angelica	*Angelica sylvestris*
Daisy	*Bellis perennis*
Scentless mayweed	*Matricaria inodora*
Autumnal hawkbit	*Leontodon autumnalis*
Sea milkwort	*Glaux maritima*
Buck's-horn plantain	*Plantago coronopus*
Sea pink	*Armeria maritima*
Orache	*Atriplex babingtonii*
Sorrel	*Rumex acetosa*
Cotton grass	*Eriophorum angustifolium*
Needle sedge	*Eleocharis (Scirpus) palustris*
Needle club rush	*Eleocharis (Scirpus) acicularis*
Tufted sedge	*Carex goodenowii*
Yorkshire fog	*Holcus lanatus*
Matgrass	*Nardus stricta*
Red fescue	*Festuca rubra*
Meadow grass	*Poa pratensis*
Adder's tongue	*Ophioglossum vulgatum*
Sandspurrey	*Spergularia salina*
Yarrow	*Achillea millefolium*
Eyebright	*Euphrasia officinalis*
Orache	*Atriplex patula*
Curled dock	*Rumex crispus*
Knotweed	*Polygonum aviculare*
Broad-leaved dock	*Rumex obtusifolius*

Jointed rush	*Juncus articulatus*
Toad rush	*Juncus bufonius*
Creeping bent grass	*Agrostis stolonifera*
Annual poa grass	*Poa annua*
Decumbent triodia	*Sieglingia decumbens*

ST KILDA FLORA

The flora of St Kilda island itself is characteristic of that of the Outer Hebrides in general, although several plant species in the St Kilda list are not given as growing in the island-chain. It can be classed as maritime Alpine or sub-Alpine flora. Perhaps the most remarkable point about the St Kilda flora is the low station at which some decidedly Alpine plants are found. The island is in the same latitude as Ben Wyvis in Ross-shire yet plants found on this mountain mass at 3,000 ft are found in St Kilda at 500 ft. Perhaps this is the more remarkable in view of the fact that there is an almost complete absence of Alpine or Arctic conditions as regards elevation and climate. The latter, for the latitude, is exceptionally mild. An insular or maritime situation is often observed to have this effect on Alpine vegetation, probably from the frequent mists and consequent diminished sunshine, and also perhaps from the comparative want of competition that would elsewhere keep them to their hill fastnesses and the coldness of the heights. The high proportion of rushes and sedges give a further Alpine character to the St Kilda plant list.

The vegetation of St Kilda is simple but luxuriant. The meadowlands between the shore and the village have thick swards of grass with admixtures of clover and bush vetch. In this area the soil is deep, fine, well-drained and contains a dense population of earthworms. The flora includes many of the plants of hill ground: sheep's fescue (*festuca ovina*), heather (*calluna*), bell heather (*erica cinerea*), blaeberry (*vaccinium myrtillus*), cowberry (*vaccinium vitis-idaea*). On the high slopes of the island are found dwarf willow (*salix herbacea*), primrose (*primula vulgaris*), honeysuckle (*lonicera periclymenum*), lady fern (*athyrium-filix-foemina*), and dandelion (*taraxacum palustre*). The maritime flora is rather

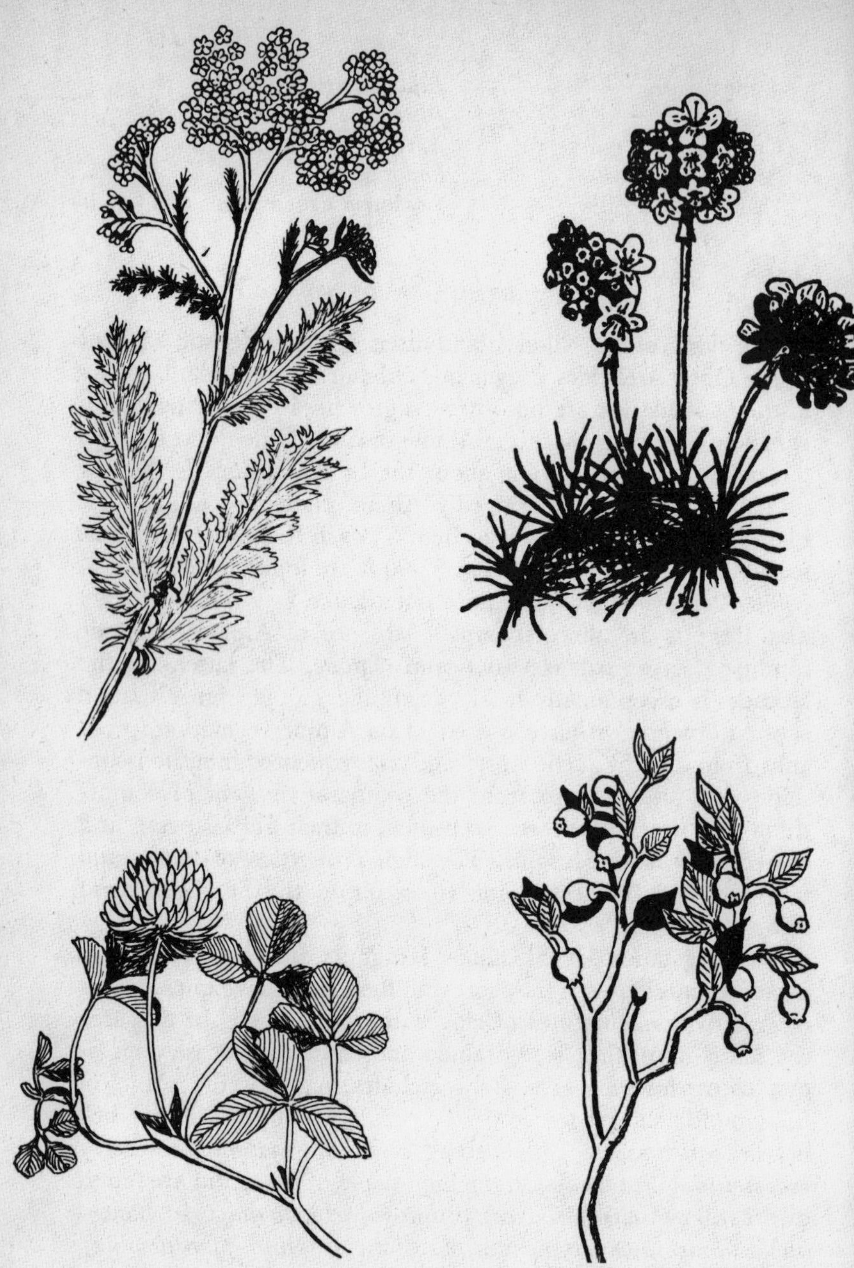

Island plants: yarrow (upper left), sea pink or thrift (upper right), Dutch clover (lower left), whortleberry (lower right)

poor, the reason being that the gabbro rock does not support other than the more common maritime plants, sea pink, sea milkwort, orache, sorrel, and sea pearlwort, all of which are found on North Rona. The turf and green vegetation on the other islands in the St Kilda group, being smaller in area, contains fewer species. In many places, the flying spray from the sea has produced a type of salting vegetation.

ST KILDA INSECTS

There are no bumble bees on St Kilda. This lack is made up in disturbing quantity by the myriads of earwigs and beetles which are to be found around the deserted villages and among the small cleits, or stone-built storehouses, higher up the slopes towards Oseval and Conachair. Midges, the curse and plague of the western Highlands of Scotland, are present in no small force on the island. The ant (*myrmica ruginodis*) is also present. Some 130 species of beetle have been found, though there are no species peculiar to the island. Butterflies, which are not numerous, include Painted Ladies (*pyrameis cardui*) and Tortoiseshell (*vanessa urticae*). The species of spiders found are those common to the mainland of Scotland.

ST KILDA FAUNA

Justifiably, it is the fauna of St Kilda which has attracted the greatest interest, more so now that the island, after some four decades of desertion, has been allowed to revert to its former natural state where characteristic species might find the right kind of environmental conditions in which to further evolve. In the St Kilda house and field mice is shown the ability of a remote island to produce differentiated races of animals. It is supposed that the house mouse (*mus musculus muralis*) was introduced into the island within historical times. The long-tailed field mouse (*apodemus sylvaticus hirtensis*) is undoubtedly a relic of an earlier age. The habitat of the house mouse was, while the island was populated by *homo sapiens*, around the village's houses except, strangely, the Post Office. After the population withdrew from the island in 1930, there was speculation as to the subsequent fate of the species. In 1933 the total population of house mice did not exceed twenty-five head. Since 1938 the species has been extinct. It is thought that the extinction was due to two factors: the large number of cats left on the island in 1930 and the species being unable to survive without the normal trappings associated with the island's firesides.

The St Kilda field mouse is rather larger than the type specimen and is sometimes inclined to be brown or yellowish underneath. The upper surface of its coat is a warm reddish brown. It is a mainly nocturnal animal. It feeds largely on grass and is found almost wholly below 400 ft. When mature, the mouse weighs twice that of its mainland counterpart; it has a larger ear and hindfoot. The mouse also occurs on Dun. There has been a small increase in the number of mating pairs since evacuation.

The other species of St Kilda fauna which is unique is the Soay sheep. This land mammal is a primitive breed of uncertain origin, although believed to be directly descended from an early stage in the domestication of the wild mouflon. Soay island is their last native habitat in Britain, and where they live in a half-wild state. Remains of the breed have been found in prehistoric settlements on the European mainland and in the middens or refuse pits of the Roman Fort at Newstead, near Melrose on the Scottish Borders.

The existence of the species in St Kilda today is attributed to the slow rate of improvement in the stock in the past: partly the result of the small size of flocks, coupled with poor communications. It is not known at what date the breed reached St Kilda. Tradition says that a Viking named Calum brought in the first sheep but there is evidence to suggest that the sheep were contemporary with prehistoric settlements in the Hebrides long before the Norsemen began their ascendancy in the islands of Scotland. Probably the first description of the Soay sheep is that of Boece (1527) who said that 'beyond Hirta there is another, uninhabited, isle (Soay). In it are certain wild beasts not very different from sheep. The hair is long and "tallie" (drab) neither like the wool of sheep nor goat'. Boece also said that on Hirta itself there was a breed of sheep with large horns and a long tail. In 1578 Bishop

Leslie made a reference to the sheep on St Kilda as being 'large animals, neither sheep nor goat, neither have they wool like a sheep nor hair like a goat, but something between the two'.

Martin Martin (1697) says of the breed: 'the number of sheep commonly maintained in St Kilda, and the two adjacent isles, does not exceed 2,000. Generally they are speckled, some white, some philamort (yellow-brown) and are of a common size; they do not resemble goats in any respect, as Buchanan was informed, except in their horns, which are extraordinarily large, particularly those in the lesser isles'. It is suggested by Ryder in *Scottish Studies* (1968) that the mention of white indicates the introduction of improved sheep, though the characteristic large horns remained.

Martin also mentions that the island of Soay offered grazing for some 500 sheep which were hunted by the St Kildans. Each ewe had two or three lambs at a birth; they lambed once each year. Martin attributed the prolificacy of the breed to the fact that the sheep were never milked, which is unlikely to have been the true reason.

MacAulay (1764) also stated that Soay supported 500 sheep; the animals were the property of the steward and were difficult to catch. He estimated that there were 100 sheep on Hirta, which were of the 'smallest kind' with short, coarse wool. Boreray was said to support 400 cast ewes from Hirta. H. J. Elwes in an article in the *Scottish Naturalist* (1912) quotes Donald Ferguson, who was ground officer on St Kilda for some twenty years, as saying that there had been no sheep with four horns during that time. This is a reference to the recurring observation that sheep with multiple horns were common through the centuries. Ferguson also said that the laird used to claim every seventh ewe, and every second ram, and put them on Soay, his preserve, and they were hunted once a year for their wool. At that time there were not less than 300 sheep on Soay: half were dark brown, half pale brown. At present, only about a quarter of the total stock are pale. Some of the light sheep have dark patches, and some of the dark animals have white marks, particularly on the face; occasional light sheep with white facial markings are still found on St Kilda. Ferguson also stated that in his time the Soay sheep were gradually becoming smaller, which is of interest in view of the large size mentioned by sixteenth-century writers.

The Soay sheep has been associated with the Northern Short-tail type of Scandinavia. Modern Icelandic sheep have a horn angle which is similar to that of the Soay. The present animals are short-haired, small in size and have long legs which give them a goat-like movement. The horns of the ram beast lift well up from the head and take a full, wide curve. The wool of the sheep is soft and has a tendency to rub off in late winter and early spring. The tail is short, triangular and without wool. The characteristic feature, which distinguishes them from the usual breeds in Britain, which are generally of Asiatic origin, is the dished or concave face and the width of the cranium compared with other facial measurements. The true Soay sheep were formerly confined to the islands of Soay and Dun, and were the sole property of MacLeod of MacLeod. The St Kildans themselves reared a mixed lot of sheep.

In 1932, two years after the evacuation, about 100 of the stock resident on Soay were taken and landed on St Kilda, where they are now carefully preserved. Estimates put the present total stock in the region of 1,500 head, of which St Kilda has about 1,100; the remainder is on Soay and on Boreray. These sheep, as might be expected on the island terrain, are extremely agile and active; they bound like sure-footed mountain goats along narrow cliff-edges and across steep grassy slopes which fall to the sea some hundreds of feet below. The sheep have been subjected to a detailed study by a team of scientists organised by the Nature Conservancy.

Though the Atlantic grey seal is common in the waters of St Kilda, it does not breed anywhere in the island group, the high cliffs defeating such a purpose. The low reaches of North Rona are the nearest breeding grounds, as are some of the islands in the Sound of Harris.

ST KILDA BIRDS

St Kilda possesses a unique species of wren: the St Kilda wren (*troglodytes hirtensis*). This bird was first mentioned by Martin

Martin in 1695 and then by MacAulay in 1764. It is slightly larger than its mainland counterpart. The nape and the head are a uniform grey brown; the rest of the upper parts are a bright brown. The under parts are pale. Barring is more pronounced and there is a white superciliary stripe. The bird's song is sweeter and less shrill than in the mainland form. It was this wren's uniqueness which nearly killed it off. When the ornithologist Seebohm first noted the bird as an important sub-species in 1884 it became a focal point of interest, particularly with hunters. By 1888, the wren was almost extinct, raids by egg collectors and amateur taxidermists having brought the numbers to a dangerously low level. But in 1904, Parliament passed the special Wild Birds Protection (St Kilda) Act, specifically designed to protect both the St Kilda wren and Leach's fork-tail petrel. In subsequent years the numbers of the species increased. Present estimates give some 100 breeding pairs, most of which are concentrated on Hirt. The bird is, by preference, a dweller in the cliffs occupied by puffins and fulmars.

In 1968, it was announced by the Advisory Committee on the Protection of Birds for Scotland that the St Kilda wren was considered to be in no danger of extinction or diminution. The bird has now been removed from the top-priority category of protected birds in Britain.

Not so fortunate was the now-extinct great auk or garefowl (*pinguinus impennis*). This bird was large and unable to fly; it laid a single egg. Its flesh was delicious, its oil was widely used for lamps, and the feathers were a useful source of cash. It was widely hunted in North America and became extinct there early in the nineteenth century. In Scotland it was already in decline in the seventeenth. Inevitably it was to be found only on the more remote islands of the Hebrides. The last auk was caught and killed in St Kilda in 1840, its captors being unaware of its identity. The species now remains in a stuffed and inanimate form in a few museums throughout the world.

The seabirds which now breed and find safe haven in St Kilda have no fear of extinction. The island contains the world's largest gannetry and the colonies of fulmar and puffin are more than significant for survival of the species. The gannet or solan goose (*sula bassana*) was once a source of economic return on the Hebridean outliers. It formed a principal source of human food. It was used as dog and cattle food in winter. Gannet's grease was highly valued for its medicinal properties, being regarded as a sure-fire cure for catarrh and gout. It was also used as a lubricant and considered excellent for treating boots, and for smearing sheep. Nor were the feathers neglected. They were used as stuffing for cheap pillows, cushions and feather beds. It was estimated that the feathers from 240 young gannets were required to make up one bed.

It is not surprising that the annual slaughtering of gannets in the British Isles (St Kilda, Sulasgeir, Bass Rock, Noss and Mermaness in the Shetlands, and Lundy Island) eventually led to either the extinction of the species or the serious reduction in the numbers of breeding pairs to below the limit for continued survival. So far as the British gannetries as a whole were concerned, however, the slaughtering which took place each year did not seriously affect the population which was well able to make good the loss each season.

Since the beginning of the twentieth century, when other sources of material to replace feathers and bird oil became readily available, the birds have been left to breed and multiply. The present gannetry on the island group of St Kilda contains about 17,000 breeding pairs.

Of the birds of the auk tribe, the razorbill, the puffin, the guillemot, the puffin is by far the most numerous. This bird (*uria aalge aalge*), which prefers to live in tunnels underneath a good turf, was also once the target of the St Kildans who could catch some 400 in one day and many thousands annually. One recent estimate suggests some 4,000,000 puffins exist between the main islands in the group. The guillemot nests on cliff edges and is not so numerous as the puffin. In comparatively fewer numbers is the razorbill (*alca torca*) which tends to live in holes in the cliff faces.

Other seabirds found on St Kilda include gulls, kittiwakes, fulmars, Manx shearwaters, storm petrels, and Leach's fork-tailed petrels. At one time, before 1878, the fulmar bred only in St Kilda, but it has since spread outwards to other breeding stations. The present population is in the region of 20,000.

Many migrant birds find St Kilda a useful stopping-off place. This has resulted in many unusual sightings by visiting naturalists. More common birds recorded include spotted redshanks, green sandpipers, starlings and an occasional turtle-dove. W. Eagle Clarke's *Studies in Bird Migration* (1912) shows the real wealth of species which take advantage of these islands in their spring and autumn movements.

NORTH RONA SEALS

The Atlantic grey seal is one of the rarest of the world's seal species, with a total population of around 45,000. A quarter of these live between Iceland and the Baltic, with a few on the coast of Canada. The number on North Rona is about 9,000. The grey seal has been protected since 1914; before that date it had been hunted nearly to extinction. Since the Bill for its protection was introduced, its numbers have increased steadily and it is now colonising new rocks such as the more accessible ones in the St Kilda group. Under legislative protection it has multiplied considerably on North Rona, which is its greatest stronghold. In recent years, scientists of the Nature Conservancy have had many opportunities to study the seal population there. One of their annual tasks has been to catch and brand some of the 2,000 seals born on North Rona each year to try and trace their movements. (The mortality rate for pups varies from 15 to 25 per cent). Branding and tagging has proved that young seals disperse widely when they leave North Rona. Recoveries have been obtained from Iceland, the Faroes, the coast of Norway, St Kilda and north-east Scotland.

APPENDIX B

ISLAND PLACENAMES

MANY of the names given to the landscape and seascape aspects of the islands in this book reflect both Norse and Gaelic elements; this is characteristic of names in the Western Isles and on the western seaboard of Scotland. In particular, aspects of the land scene, as seen from seaward, are predominantly Norse; which might be expected in view of the seafaring adventurous spirit of the mariners from Scandinavia.

There has always been some difficulty in arriving at the correct derivation of a placename. For a long time it was a matter of guesswork, however intelligent. Nowadays, the professional etymologist is needed to solve the mystery of names which have been corrupted through centuries of use and misuse. Added to a thorough knowledge of philology, a clear understanding of phonetics is also needed. Topographical information is also important. The processes called 'assimilation' and 'dissimilation' often alter a word so completely that the present form is quite different from the original.

One of the most common suffixes in the islands' coast names is 'ness', or, in its Gaelicised form, *nish* or *nis*. This is Old Norse *nes* = a headland; it is sometimes used to denote the extremity of the headland.

Small pinpoints of rock lying off a large land-mass may seem insignificant; lying off a small island-mass, however, they become important aspects of the seascape. The Norse word for island is *ey*, expressed in Gaelic by *aidh*. One of the Flannan Islands is Soray, also written Soridh. This is commonly thought to mean 'farewell island' from the Gaelic *soraidh*. The island's name may, however, be derived from its height above the sea, in which case a Norse derivation could be ascribed to make 'high island', which is common to the derivation ascribed to Harris in the Long Island. Instances of Gaelic in the Flannans are seen in *Eilean a' Ghobha* (Smith's Island), and in *Eilean Tighe* (House Island).

As might be expected from living in an island environment closely circumscribed by the coastline, personal elements are conspicuously present in many of the placenames. On North Rona there is *Geodha Mairi* (Mary's Creek), *Leac Iain Tailleir* (rock-slab of Iain the Tailor), *Cladach Cro Iain Dheirg* (shore-land of the cattle of Iain the Red). Some names indicate a long-past religious association: on the Monach Isles there is *Tigh na Croice* (House of the Cross).

'The Irte, which is agreed to be under Circius and on the out-skirts of the world, beyond which there is found no land in these bounds'. This was Fordun's description (*c* 1400) of the St Kilda group of islands. The name 'Irte' was the old name and appears in various forms such as *Hirt* and *Hirta*. The origin of *Hirt* has been laid at a Celtic door by Prof W. J. Watson who contended the name meant death or gloom, in keeping with a land of spirits beyond the far horizon and with the Gaelic *h-Iar-Tir* = west-land. In later centuries, the name St Kilda became more common. However, the first documented mention of the island is *Hyrt*, in a Charter granted by John, Lord of the Isles, to his son Reginald, and confirmed by King Robert the Second after the middle of the fourteenth century. 'St Kilda' itself is also a source of bother to etymologists. Kilda, from the Norse *kelda*, meaning a well, first occurs in a map dated 1558. Another origin is thought to be Culdee, the name given to the early Christian missionaries of the Celtic Church in Scotland. The Dutch fishing activity in the western seas during the seventeenth century led to a Dutch map-maker adding the word 'saint' to his maps of the area. No saint of the name Kilda has ever existed, however, and the origin of the name by which the island group is known today is as ghostly as the islands themselves.

Soay is derived from the Norse *saudhr*, meaning sheep isle; there are many such names in the Western Isles. Boreray is the north isle. Stac Lee is the hoary rock, and Stac an Armin is the stack of the warrior.

The following short list of names and their elements is not

intended to be comprehensive but only a useful guide to the more obvious placenames of the Hebridean Outlier islands.

ST KILDA

Stac an Armin Stack of the Warrior
Rudh Briste Wreck point of the breaking
Gob na Tarnanach Mouth of the loud sounds
Gealgo Short geo or creek
Udraclete Stony ridge
Sgarbhstac Stack of the cormorants
Creagan na Rubhaig Bana Rocks of the white hemp thongs (climbing?)
Am Plaistair Place of splashing (sea-wash)
Geo Ruadh Red geo or creek
Gob a' Ghaill Mouth of the rock
Cnoc Glas Grey hill
Sgeir Mac Righ Lochlainn Rock of the King of Norway's son
Stac Dona Bad stack
Geo Chalum M'Mhurich Creek of Calum MacMhurich (Murchison)
The Cambir Place of burial
Geo na h-Airde Creek of the height
Loch a' Ghlinne Glen loch
Sgeir Dhomnaill Donald's rock
Stac a Langa Long stack
Rudha Ghill The boy's point
Sgeirnan Sgarbh Rocks of the cormorants
Oiseval Steep sloping hill
Rudha an Uisge Point of the water
Geo dh' Clann Neill Creek of Clan Neill
Seilg Geo Hunting creek
Mullach Sgar Ruaival Summit of the clefted red hill
Rudha Mhuirich Point of the MacMhurichs
Mullach Mor Big summit

NORTH RONA

Lisgear Mhor Big grey rock
Sgor na Lice Moire Rock of the big slabs
Leac Mhor Fianuis Big rock-slab of Fianuis
Geodha a' Stoth Creek of steam (sea-drift)
Geodha Mairi Mary's creek

Sron na Caorach Sheep's nose
Leac Iain Tailleir Rock-slab of Iain the Tailor
Geodha na Breatuinn Creek of the Britons (Bretons?)
Pollan Uisg Little water pool
Stac a' Phriosuin Prison stack
Leac na Sgrob Rock-slab of the scratches
Buaile na' Sgrath Herding place of the lowing or bleating
Bogh' a Mheadhon La Sunken rock (middle distance)
Caolas Loba Sgeir Rock of the narrows or strait
Caolas Harsgeir Strait of the sea-rock
Harsgeir Sea-rock
Marcasgeo Sea-drift creek
Cladach Cro Iain Dheirg Shoreland of the cattle of Iain the Red
Leacan 's Iar West rock-slabs
Cro Mhic Iain Choinnich Cattle of Kenneth's Iain (MacKenzie?)
Geodha nan Gall Creek of the strangers
Geodha Blatha Mor Creek of the big sea
Geodha Blatha Beag Creek of the little sea
Geodha Leis Leeward creek
Pol a' Chleirich Pool of the cleric (priest)
Geodh' an Tuill Creek of the running tide
Lisgear Grey rock
Boghanan Sunken rocks

SULASGEIR
Bogha Corr Sunken rock
Boghannan s' Iar West sunken rocks
Pol a' Chaitainich Pool of the (Caithness-men?)
Thamna Sgeir Tongue rock
Geodha Phuill Bhain Creek of the white rounded stones
Geodh' a' Bhun Mhoir Creek at the river mouth
Sgeir an Teampuill Temple rock
Bealach an t-Suidhe Glen of the resting-place
Creag Trithaiga Rock of the (three houses?)
Sron na Lice Nose of the rock-slab
Pairc a's Iar West park
Cnap Geodha Blatha Beag Little hill of the creek of the little sea
Tigh Mhaoldonuich House of Mhaoldonuich (*Maol* = votary) probably hermit
Geodha Blatha Mor Creek of the big sea
Lamha Cleit Lamb's cliff

Da Bogha Lamha Cleit Two sunken rocks at the lamb's cliff
Bogha Leathainn Broad sunken rock
Gralisgeir Grey rock

FLANNAN ISLES
Gealtaire Mor Big white (bright or clear) land
Gealtaire Beag Small white land
Dearc na Sgeir Rock cave
Sron na Faing Nose (promontory) of the vulture
Eilean Tighe House Island
Hamasgeir Ocean rock
Geodh' an Truillich Creek of the (worthless person?)
Skiopageo Creek of the ship (skiff)
Eilean Mor Big Island
Tom na Geodha Hill of the creek
Meall Meadhonach Middle Hill
Soray Farewell Island (?) has the terminal *ay* (*ey*, Norse) = island
Sgeir Toman Hill rock
Roareim Anguish Point (*rudha doruinn*)
Poll nan Ron Pool of the seals
Brona Cleit Protuberance (belly) of the reef
Eilean a' Ghobha Smith's Island

MONACH ISLES
Stogay Rudder Island (Stoc = stock of a ship's rudder)
Ru' na Marbh Death Point
Port Roidh Seal Harbour
An Ceann Ear East head
Cladh na Bleide Burying place
Giortinish Edge of the ness or promontory
Sgeir Mhor Big rock
Crois Shithinis Ness of the Peace cross
An Ceann Iar West head
Tigh na Croice House of the Cross
Hearnish East Point
Sillay Rainy Island
na Diurabegs Small hard (difficult) rocks

BIBLIOGRAPHY

Many writers throughout the centuries have written about the Hebridean islands. Some speak of an island's personality. R. L. Stevenson said:

> On all this part of the coast . . . (the Outer Hebrides) these great granite rocks that I have spoken of go down together in troops to the sea, like cattle on a summer's day. There they stand, for all the world like their neighbours ashore; only salt water sobbing between them instead of the quiet earth, and clots of sea-pink blooming on their sides instead of heather, and the great sea-conger to wreathe about the base of them instead of the poisonous viper of the land.

Some writers have written descriptions of their visits to the islands and fallen into the trap of comparing the environment of the island community with that of an urbanised society. Others have extolled the 'freedom' of an island community from the various influences which impose stresses and strains on urbanised communities—yet they would have probably thought twice about choosing an island as a place in which to live permanently. Perhaps those deeply interested in natural history have done most justice to the islands and their communities, for the reason that their specific interest allowed only cogent observations of the human element into their writings. But missionaries, teachers, naturalists, archaeologists, tourists, factors and owners, and journalists have all contributed to the relevant literature.

The first writer on the outlying islands of the Hebrides, who has left a record of his work, was Sir Donald Monro, High Dean of the Isles; he wrote in 1549. His conceptions of size and distance leave much to be desired, but his work tells us much of life in these islands. Next came the 'Gentleman from Skye', Martin Martin. His book was first published in 1698 and is still a much-thumbed volume on library shelves. His work was detailed and accurate, and is invaluable to the student of natural history today.

John MacCulloch, the 'Stone Doctor', was a fluent geologist who travelled among the Western Isles between 1811 and 1821. His descriptions are often rather high-flown and for natural history he is secondary to Martin, but his literary eloquence filled four volumes in 1824.

Enthusiasm is the keynote of the band of nineteenth-century naturalists, headed by Harvie-Brown and who are perpetuated in the *Vertebrate Fauna of Scotland* series. These include J. Swinburne, T. E. Buckley, M. E. Heddle, and R. M. Barrington. The work deals not only with natural history but acts as a useful guidebook and includes some of the first photographs ever taken in Scotland's remote small islands.

The present century has also seen its full share of visitors to the islands. J. Wilson Dougal, the geologist, T. S. Muir, the ecclesiologist, and J. Sands, the tourist, have all made their contribution. In particular one must mention Malcolm Stewart who visited most of the remoter islands and rocks and recorded his observations in a book and in papers. Stewart was also responsible for gathering together a group of modern scientific papers on St Kilda and publishing them as a volume. In later years, no doubt encouraged by Stewart's work, writers like Robert Atkinson and Frank Fraser Darling fulfilled lifelong ambitions to land on the islands and have left accounts which are most absorbing to read.

With the exception of St Kilda, however, the bibliography of the Hebridean Outliers is not particularly extensive. North Rona ceased to be socially significant when it became deserted, an event which occurred before its many visitors had recorded their impressions. Sulasgeir has been written about in the contexts of its geology, natural history and the social link it had, and still has, with the north of Lewis. The range of the Flannans' literature is similar to that of Sulasgeir. The Monach Isles have been the subject of a novel, but otherwise have not been the specific aim of literary ambitions. St Kilda, perhaps because of the size of its community and its distance from the west coast of Scotland, and thus civilisation, has been subjected to the close scrutiny of visitors. The result has been a spate of words in the form of official reports, general articles of an informative and entertaining nature, personal reports and documents, novels, sketches, newspaper items, topographical and social descriptions and so on.

The following bibliographical list of some 170 titles is reasonably comprehensive and indicates the extreme range of topics dealt with. Though some titles are concerned specifically with St Kilda, others of a more general nature deal, sometimes *in passim*, with the other Hebridean islands. Many of the titles, of the books in particular, are out of print and are available only in the older-established public libraries, in University libraries and in private collections of Highland books. Occasionally these titles crop up, often unexpectedly, in the book lists of second-hand book dealers; though a reasonable price must be paid. Even so, for the enthusiast, a price of some 6 gns (£6·30) is not too much for the first edition (1878) of Seton's *St Kilda—Past and Present.*

The titles marked with an asterisk are of particular interest to those readers of the present book who wish to study the Hebridean Outliers in greater depth. Their various authors viewed the islands through a very wide spectrum of interests and have recorded not only facts, but their impressions. Often they had a genuine concern for the islanders with whom they invariably made fast friends. Reading through the centuries from, say, the eighteenth century to the last poignant farewell to St Kilda in 1930, one begins to realise how and why these outer Hebridean islands cast their spell, so strong even now through the medium of the printed page, but especially so during those last decades when the whole world seemed to beat an inquisitive trail to St Kilda's very doorstep.

BOOKS

ADMIRALTY. *West Coast of Scotland Pilot.* London, 1934

*ATKINSON, ROBERT. *Island Going.* London, 1949

*BEVERIDGE, E. *North Uist: Archaeology and Topography.* Edinburgh, 1911

BROUGHAM, LORD. 'Tour in the Western Isles, including St Kilda in 1799'; from *The Life and Times of Henry, Lord Brougham,* 1871, Vol II

*BUCHAN, A. *A Description of St Kilda.* Edinburgh, 1727

BUCHANAN, J. L. *Travels in the Western Hebrides.* London, 1793

CARMICHAEL, A. *Carmina Gadelica.* 5 Vols, Edinburgh, 1923–54

CARRUTHERS, R. *The Highland Note-book: or Sketches and Anecdotes.* Inverness, 1843

CLARKE, E. D. *The Life and Remains of Edward Daniel Clarke.* Ed. Rev Willian Otter. 2 Vols, London, 1825. 2nd edition contains 'Visit to St Kilda in 1727'

*CONNELL, R. *St Kilda and the St Kildans.* London, 1887

CROMARTIE, SIR GEORGE MACKENZIE, 1st EARL OF. 'An Account of Hirta and Rona (1680)'. In Monro's *Description of the Western Isles,* 1774

CUMMING, GORDON, C. F. *In the Hebrides.* London, 1883

DALGLEISH, DR. *A Maid of Rona. c* 1773

*DARLING, F. FRASER. *A Naturalist on Rona.* London, 1939

*DARLING, F. FRASER. *Island Years.* London, 1940

DARLING, F. FRASER. *Island Farm.* London, 1944

*DARLING, F. FRASER. *Natural History in the Highlands and Islands.* London, 1947

DOUGAL, J. W. *Island Memories.* Edinburgh, 1937

DUCKWORTH, C. L. D. AND LANGMUIR, G. E. *West Highland Steamers.* Prescot, 1967

FERGUSON, M. *Ramblers in Skye*; with a sketch of a trip to St Kilda, 1885

GORDON, SETON. *Islands of the West.* London, 1933

GRIMBLE, I. AND THOMSON, D. S. *The Future of the Highlands.* London, 1968

HARVIE-BROWN, J. A. AND BUCKLEY, T. E. *Vertebrate Fauna of the Outer Hebrides.* Edinburgh, 1889

*HEATHCOTE, J. N. *St Kilda.* London, 1900

*KEARTON, R. *With Nature and a Camera.* London, 1902

KENNEDY, J. *The 'Apostle' of the North*: The Life and Labours of the Rev Dr John MacDonald. London, 1866

LAWSON, R. *A Flight to St Kilda in July, 1902.* Paisley

LEWIS, M. *Island of Disaster.* (Fiction with background of Heisgeir).

LOGIE, D. W. *An Account of a Trip from Stirling to St Kilda, 12–17 August, 1889.* Stirling, 1889

*MACAULAY, K. *Voyage to St Kilda.* London, 1764

MACCULLOCH, J. *Description of the Western Islands.* London, 1824

MACDONALD, J. *General View of the Agriculture of the Hebrides.* Edinburgh, 1811

MACINTOSH, C. FRASER. 'Parish of Harris: St Kilda', contained in *Antiquarian Notes.* Inverness, 1897

*MacKay, J. A. *St Kilda, its Posts and Communications.* 1963
MacKenzie, O. *A Hundred Years of Life in the Highlands.* 1921
MacKenzie, W. C. *The Lady of Hirta*: A Tale of the Isles. Paisley, 1905
MacLean, L. *Sketches of the Island of St Kilda.* Glasgow, 1838
Map of the Islands of St Kilda, Borrera, etc, etc, taken August 1899 (by Robert Campbell). Engraved in Arrowsmith's *Memoir Relative to the Map of Scotland.* 1823
*Martin, M. *A Late Voyage to St Kilda.* London, 1698. Also Stirling, 1934
*Martin, M. *Description of the Western Islands of Scotland.* London, 1705. Also Glasgow, 1884, and Stirling, 1934
Mercey, F. 'Visit to St Kilda', in *Scotia: Souvenirs et recit de Voyages*, 1842
Monipennie, J. *History of Scotland.* Edinburgh, 1751
Monro, Sir Donald. *A Description of the Western Isles of Scotland called Hybrides, c* 1549. Stirling, 1934
Muir, T. S. *Ecclesiological Notes on Some of the Islands of Scotland.* Edinburgh, 1885
O'Dell, A. C. and Walton, K. *The Highlands and Islands of Scotland.* London, 1962
Ogilvie, J. *'Rona: a Poem in Seven Books'.* London, 1777
Old Statistical Account of Scotland. Edinburgh, 1796
Sands, J. *Out of the world; or, Life in St Kilda.* Edinburgh, Revised edition, 1878
Scott, W. R. *Report to the Board of Agriculture on Home Industries in the Highlands and Islands.* (Parliamentary Paper). Edinburgh, 1914
Scottish Mountaineering Club. *The Islands of Scotland.* Edinburgh, 1952
*Seton, G. *St Kilda—Past and Present.* Edinburgh, 1878
Shand, A. I. *The Lady Grange.* London, 1897
Sibbald, Sir Robert. 'An Account of Hirta and Rona'. Printed in Pinkerton's *General Collection of Voyages and Travels*, Vol III. London, 1809
Smith, R. A. *Visit to St Kilda in the 'Nyanza'.* 1879
*Steel, T. *The Life and Death of St Kilda.* Edinburgh, 1965
*Stewart, M. *Ronay.* Oxford, 1933
Svensson, R. *Lonely Isles.* London, 1954
Thom, A. *Megalithic Sites in Britain.* Oxford, 1967

THOMPSON, Francis. *Harris Tweed: The Story of a Hebridean Industry*. Newton Abbot, 1969

*WILLIAMSON, K. AND MORTON BOYD, J. *St Kilda Summer*. London, 1960

WILSON, J. 'St Kilda in 1841'. In his *Voyage Round the Coasts of Scotland*. Edinburgh, 1842

ARTICLES IN PERIODICALS

Abbreviations:

Ann Scot Nat Hist—*Annals* of the Scottish Natural History Society
Brit Birds—British Birds
Brit & For Med-Chir Rev—British & Foreign Medico-Chirurgical Review
Brit Med Jour—British Medical Journal
Caledonian Med Jour—Caledonian Medical Journal
Edin Mag—Edinburgh Magazine
Entomol Mon Mag—Entomological Monthly Magazine
Geog Jour—Geographical Journal
Geol Mag—Geological Magazine
Jour Anim Ecol—Journal of Animal Ecology
Jour B'ham Nat Hist & Phil Soc—*Journal* of the Birmingham Natural History & Philosophical Society
Jour Bot—Journal of Botany
Jour Ecol—Journal of Ecology
New Phil Jour—New Philosophical Journal
Proc Nat Hist Soc Glasgow—*Proceedings* of the Natural History Society of Glasgow
Proc Roy Phys Soc Edin—*Proceedings* of the Royal Physical Society of Edinburgh
Proc Soc Antiq Scot—*Proceedings* of the Society of Antiquaries of Scotland
Proc Zoo Soc Lon—*Proceedings* of the Zoological Society of London.
Scot Geog Mag—Scottish Geographical Magazine
Scot Mount Club Jour—Scottish Mountaineering Club Journal
Scot Nat—Scottish Naturalist
Trans Bot Soc Edin—*Transactions* of the Botanical Society of Edinburgh
Trans Geo Soc Edin—*Transactions* of the Geological Society of Edinburgh

Trans High & Agric Soc of Scot—*Transactions* of the Highland and Agricultural Society of Scotland
Trans Liverpool Biol Soc—*Transactions* of the Liverpool Biological Society
Trans Nat Hist Soc of Northumberland—*Transactions* of the Natural History Society of Northumberland
Trans Roy Phil Soc—*Transactions* of the Royal Philosophical Society
Trans Roy Soc Edin—*Transactions* of the Royal Society of Edinburgh

AINSLIE, J. A. AND ATKINSON, R. 'On the Breeding Habits of Leach's fork-tailed Petrel'. *Brit Birds*, 30, 1937
AINSLIE, J. A. AND ATKINSON, R. 'Summer Bird Notes from North Rona'. *Scot Nat*, 1937
ANON. 'Life in St Kilda', *Chambers Journal*, Vol. LIV, 1880
ATKINSON, G. C. 'An Account of an Expedition to St Kilda in 1831'. *Trans* Nat Hist Soc of Northumberland. 1832
ATKINSON, R. 'Natural History Notes from Certain Scottish Islands—North Rona, the Flannan Isles, Handa Island'. *Scot Nat*, 1938
ATKINSON, R. 'Notes on the Botany of North Rona and Sulasgeir'. *Trans* Bot Soc Edin, Vol 33, 1940
BAILLIE, LADY (of Polkemmet). 'A Short Visit to St Kilda'. *Church of Scotland Missionary Record*, January 1875
BARRINGTON, R. M. 'Notes on the Flora of St Kilda'. *Jour Bot*, Vol XXIV, 1886
BARRINGTON, R. M. 'Plants observed on North Rona, July 1, 1886'. In Harvie-Brown's 'Further Notes on North Rona'. *Proc* Roy Phys Soc Edin, Vol IX, 1885
BARRINGTON, R. M. 'The Ascent of Stack-na-Biorrach'. *Alpine Journal*, Vol XXVII, *c* 1886
BENNET, A. 'The Plants of the Flannan Islands'. *Ann* Scot Nat Hist, 1907
BEDFORD, DUCHESS OF 'On Visits paid to the Island of North Rona'. *Ann* Scot Nat Hist, 1910
BOYD, J. M. 'An Expedition to Hirta'. *Scottish Field*, October 1957
BOYD, J. M. 'St Kilda in 1952'. *Scottish Field*, October 1952
BOYD, J. M., DONEY, J. M., GUNN, R. G. AND JEWELL, P. A. 'The Soay Sheep of the Island of Hirta, St Kilda. A Study of a Feral Population'. *Proc* Zoo Soc Lon, 142, 1964

BIBLIOGRAPHY

BRAZENOR, H. 'Proposed Dealer's Raid on the Birds of St Kilda and the Outer Hebrides', *Ann* Scot Nat Hist, 1908

CAMBRIDGE, O. PICKARD. 'Spiders of St Kilda'. *Ann* Scot Nat Hist, 1905

CAMERON, M. 'Our Childhood on St Kilda'. *Scots Magazine*, March 1969

CHAMBERS, W. 'The Story of Lady Grange'. *Chamber's Journal*, 4th Series, No 551, 1874

CLARKE, W. E. 'Notes on the Mice of St Kilda'. *Scot Nat*, 1914

CLARKE, W. E. 'The Wren of St Kilda'. *Scot Nat*, 1915

COCKBURN, A. M. 'The Geology of St Kilda'. *Trans* Roy Soc Edin, Vol 58, 1936

DIXON, C. 'The Ornithology of St Kilda'. *Ibis*, 5th Series, III, 1885

DONALD, S. 'North Rona'. *Scottish Field*, July 1959

DOUGAL, J. W. 'Geology of Lewis and N. Rona'. *Trans* Geol Soc Edin, XII, *c* 1930

ELLIOT, J. S. 'St Kilda and the St Kildans'. *Jour* B'ham Nat Hist & Phil Soc, I, 1895

ELLIOT, J. S. 'Observations on the Fauna of St Kilda'. *Zoologist*, XIX, 1895

ELWES, H. J. 'Bird Stations of the Outer Hebrides'. *Ibis*, 1869

ELWES, H. J. 'Notes on the Primitive Breeds of Sheep of Scotland'. *Scot Nat*, Nos 1, 2 & 3, 1912

GIBSON, A. H. 'The Phanerogamic Flora of St Kilda'. *Trans* Bot Soc Edin, Vol XIX, 1891

GIBSON, G. 'The Tragedy of St Kilda'. *Caledonian Med Jour*, April 1926

GIBSON, W. W. 'Flannan Isle'. A Poem in *Fires*, London, 1915

GRIESHEIM, A. VON 'Eine Fahrt nach St Kilda'. Deutsche Rundschau, XXII, 1899

GRIMSHAW, P. H. 'On the Diptera of St Kilda'. *Ann* Scot Nat Hist, 1907

HAMILTON, G. E. H. BARRET. 'On a Collection of Mice from St Kilda'. *Ann* Scot Nat Hist, 1906

HARRISSON, T. H. AND BUCHAN, J. N. S. 'A Field Study of the St Kildan Wren'. *Jour Anim Ecol*, 3, 1934

HARRISSON, T. H. AND BUCHAN, J. N. S. 'Further Notes on a Field Study of the St Kilda Wren'. *Scot Nat*, 1936

HARRISSON, T. H. AND LACK, D. 'The Breeding Birds of St Kilda'. *Scot Nat*, 1934

HARRISSON, T. H. AND MOY-THOMAS, J. A. 'St Kilda House Mouse'. *Nature*, 1932

HARRISSON, T. H. AND MOY-THOMAS, J. A. 'The Mice of St Kilda'. *Jour Anim Ecol*, 2, 1933

HARVIE-BROWN, J. A. 'Flannan Isles and their Bird Life'. *Proc* Nat Hist Soc Glasgow, Vol V, 1880–83

HARVIE-BROWN, J. A. 'The Islands and Rocks of Haskeir'. *Proc* Nat Hist Soc Glasgow, Vol V, 1884

HEATHCOTE, E. 'A Summer Sojourn in St Kilda'. *Good Words*, London, 1901

HEATHCOTE, J. N. 'A Map of St Kilda'. *Geog Jour*, XV, 1900

HEATHCOTE, N. 'Climbing in St Kilda'. *Scot Mount Club Jour*, Vol 6, 1900

HEWITT, C. G. 'A Contribution to the Flora of St Kilda'. *Ann* Scot Nat Hist, 1907

HEWITT, C. G. 'Some Arthroostraca and other Invertebrata from St Kilda'. *Ann* Scot Nat Hist, 1907

H. R. M. 'St Kilda'. The *Celtic Magazine*, Vol XI, Inverness, 1886

HUXLEY, J. 'Birds and Men on St Kilda'. *Geog Mag*, Vol 10, 1939

JOY, N. H. 'Notes on Coleoptera from St Kilda'. *Ann* Scot Nat Hist, 1908

LACK, D. 'Coleoptera on St Kilda in 1931'. *Entomol Mon Mag*, 67, 1931

LACK, D. 'Further Notes on Insects on St Kilda'. *Entomol Mon Mag*, 68, 1932

LACK, D. 'Notes on the Diptera of St Kilda'. *Entomol Mon Mag*, 68, 1933

LACK, D. 'Ecological Features of the Bird Faunas of British Small Islands'. *Jour Anim Ecol*, 10, 1942

LAING, D. 'Lady Grange on the Island of St Kilda'. *Proc* Soc Antiq Scot, Vol X, 1875; Vol XI, 1876

MACCALLUM, H. 'St Kilda'. *Caledonian Med Jour*, Vol VII, 1907

MACDIARMID, J. 'St Kilda and its Inhabitants'. *Trans* High & Agric Soc of Scot, Vol X, 1878

MACDONALD, C. R. 'St Kilda: its Inhabitants and the Diseases peculiar to them'. *Brit Med Jour*, II, 1886

MACDONALD, D. A. 'Eilean Heisgeir'. *Gairm* No 20, (Glasgow), 1957

MACDONALD, J. 'Journal of a visit to St Kilda, etc'. In an appendix to SPCK 'Sermon Preached by Rev W. A. Thomson, on June 6, 1822'

MACGILLIVRAY, J. 'An Account of the Island of St Kilda, chiefly with reference to its Natural History'. *New Phil Jour*, Vol XXXII, 1842

MacGregor, D. R. 'St Kilda'. *Scottish Studies*, Vol 4, 1960

MacInnes, D. J. 'The Lonely Keepers of the Flannan Light'. *Stornoway Gazette*, 2 March 1968

MacKenzie, Sir George. 'An Account of the Misfortunes of Mrs Erskine of Grange, Commonly known as Lady Grange'. *Edin Mag*, I, 1817

MacKenzie, H. R. 'St Kilda'. *Celtic Magazine*, XI, 1885

MacKenzie, J. B. 'Antiquities and Old Customs in St Kilda'. *Proc* Soc Antiq Scot, Vol XXXIX (4th Series, Vol III), 1904–5

MacKenzie, N. 'Notes on the Birds of St Kilda'. *Ann* Scot Nat Hist, 1905

Maladies de l'Ile St Kilda', 'Les. *Gazette Medical de Paris*, 11s; I. 1898

Mathieson, J. 'St Kilda'. *Scot Geog Mag*, Vol XLIV, 1928

Milner, Sir W. M. E. 'Some Account of the People of St Kilda and of the Birds of the Outer Hebrides'. *Zoologist*, VI, 1848

Mitchell, A. 'List of Accounts of Visits to St Kilda (1549–1900)', *Proc* Soc Antiq Scot, Vol XXXV, 1901

Moisley, H. A. 'The Deserted Hebrides'. *Scottish Studies*, Vol 10, 1966

Moray, Sir Robert. 'A Description of the Island of Hirta'. *Trans* Roy Phil Soc, 1678

Morgan, J. E. 'The Diseases of St Kilda'. *Brit & For Med & Chir Rev*, XXIX, 1862

Muir, T. S. and Thomas, F. W. L. 'Notice of a Beehive House in the Island of St Kilda'. *Proc* Soc Antiq Scot, Vol III, 1862

Muir, T. S. 'Incholm, Aberdour, No. Rona, Sula Sgeir : A Sketch, 1872'. *Proc* Soc Antiq Scot, Vol V, 1890

Murchison, T. M. 'Deserted Hebridean Isles : Notes and Traditions'. *Trans* Gaelic Soc Inverness, Vol XLII, 1953–59

Murray, J. 'Microscopic life of St Kilda'. *Ann* Scot Nat Hist, 1905

Nicholson, E. M. and Fisher, J. 'A Bird Census of St Kilda'. *Brit Birds*, 34, 1940

Petch, C. P. 'The Vegetation of St Kilda'. *Jour Ecol*, 21, 1933

Pickard-Cambridge, O. 'Spiders of St Kilda'. *Ann* Scot Nat Hist, 1905

Price, E. 'Voyage to St Kilda'. *Scotsman*, 21 July 1906

Ross, A. 'A Visit to the Island of St Kilda'. *Trans* Inverness Scientific Society and Field Club, Vol III, 1883–8

RYDER, M. 'The Evolution of Scottish Breeds of Sheep'. *Scottish Studies*, Vol 12, 1968

SANDS, J. 'Notes on the Antiquities of the Island of St Kilda'. *Proc* Soc Antiq Scot, Vol XII, 1876–8

STEWART, M. 'Notes on the Geology of North Rona'. *Geol Mag*, 1932

STEWART, M. 'Notes on the Geology of Sula Sgeir and the Flannan Islands'. *Geol Mag*, 1933

STEWART, M. 'Notes on the Gannetries of Sule Stack and Sula Sgeir'. *Brit Birds*, 31, 1938

STUDDY, R. 'Beyond the Hebrides'. *Scottish Field*, November 1953

SUTHERLAND, A. 'The St Kilda Flora'. *Trans* Inverness Field Club, Vol III, 1887

SWINBURNE, J. 'Notes on the Islands of Sulasgeir or North Barra and North Rona, with a list of the Birds inhabiting them'. *Proc* Roy Phys Soc Edin, Vol VIII, Pt 1, *c* 1885

TAYLOR, A. B. 'The Name "St Kilda"'. *Scottish Studies*, Vol 13, 1969

THOMAS, F. W. L. 'On Primitive Dwellings and the Hypogea of the Outer Hebrides'. *Proc* Soc Antiq Scot, Vol VII, 1867

THOMAS, F. W. L. 'Letter from St Kilda' by Miss A. Kennedy; with notes by Capt Thomas. *Proc* Soc Antiq Scot, Vol XII, 1876–8

THOMSON, D. C. 'St Kilda as it was a Century Ago'. *Scotsman*, 30 November 1957

TRAILL, J. W. H. 'The Plants of the Flannan Islands'. *Ann* Scot Nat Hist, 1905

WATERSTON, J. 'Notes on the Mice and Birds of St Kilda'. *Ann* Scot Nat Hist, 1905

WATERSTON, J. 'On Some Invertebrates from St Kilda'. *Ann* Scot Nat Hist, 1906

WATERSTON, J. AND TAYLOR, J. W. 'Land and Fresh Water Molluscs of St Kilda'. *Ann* Scot Nat Hist, 1906

WIGLESWORTH, J. 'St Kilda and its Birds'. *Trans* Liverpool Biol Soc, 1903

WILLIAMSON, K. 'Ancient St Kilda'. *Scottish Field*, March 1958

MISCELLANEOUS REPORTS, PAPERS, MSS, ETC

ANCIENT MONUMENTS, ROYAL COMMISSION ON. *Ninth Report, with*

Inventory of Monuments and Constructions in the Outer Hebrides, Skye and The Small Isles. HMSO, Edinburgh, 1928

GRANGE, LADY RACHEL. *Epistle from Lady Grange to Edward D-, Esq.* London, 1798

INVERNESS EDUCATION AUTHORITY. *Log Book of St Kilda School* (Held by the Authority in Inverness)

MACNEIL, M. 'On His Visit to St Kilda'. *Annual Report* of the Board of Supervision, 1884

PAROCHIAL REGISTERS: St Kilda, 1830-51; Marriages, 1830–49; Deaths, 1830–46. (Initially kept by Rev N. MacKenzie. Now in the Scottish Record Office, General Register House, Edinburgh)

ROSS, J. *Notes on the Island of St Kilda.* Made while a schoolmaster in St Kilda, 1887–8. (Bute Collection)

SSPCK *Minutes of Committee, c 1710.* (In the Scottish Record Office, General Register House, Edinburgh)

STEWART, M. *St Kilda Papers*, 1931. Private circulation to various libraries (total 25) in Britain.

STEWART, M. *Bibliography of the Island of St Kilda.* Private circulation

ST KILDA: Papers relating to the 1930 evacuation. (Deposited in the Scottish Record Office, General Register House, Edinburgh)

ACKNOWLEDGMENTS

I have to acknowledge the valuable help given by many people in the preparation of this book. In particular, the following have given specific assistance in varying degrees in either providing source material or illustrative matter: James McGeoch, Aviemore; Walter Aldebert, Cromarty Lighthouse; Mrs Anne Turner, Lochwinnoch; Donald MacDonald, Glasgow; Sam Longbotham, of the *Stornoway Gazette*; Mrs F. MacDonald, Fort William; and Frank Thompson, Stornoway, my father who, over a decade ago, provided a set of photographs of North Rona and Sulasgeir little knowing they would be adding an extra dimension to the text of this book.

I am also grateful to the following for permission to quote from their own works: Malcolm Stewart, *Ronay*; Frank Fraser Darling, *Island Years*; Robert Atkinson, *Island Going*; and Roland Svensson, *Lonely Isles*. My thanks are also due to the trustees of *Carmina Gadelica*.

I have finally to thank my wife who provided most of the line drawings in the book.

INDEX

Page numbers in italics indicate illustrations

I

J

K

L

M

N

O

P

R

S